D1306461

INVITATION TO A MARCH

Invitation to a March

A NEW COMEDY BY ARTHUR LAURENTS

 RANDOM HOUSE, NEW YORK

To

Richard Goldstone

INVITATION TO A MARCH *was first presented by The Theatre
Guild at The Music Box Theatre, New York City, on October
29, 1960, with the following cast:*

(IN ORDER OF APPEARANCE)

CAMILLA JABLONSKI	Celeste Holm
LILY BROWN	Madeleine Sherwood
CARY BROWN	Jeffrey Rowland
DEEDEE GROGAN	Eileen Heckart
SCHUYLER GROGAN	Tom Hatcher
NORMA BROWN	Jane Fonda
AARON JABLONSKI	James MacArthur
TUCKER GROGAN	Richard Derr

Directed by ARTHUR LAURENTS
Settings by WILLIAM PITKIN
Lighting by PAUL MORRISON
Costumes by LUCINDA BALLARD
Original music by STEPHEN SONDHEIM

The action of the play occurs on the South Shore of Long Island in the summer.

Act One

The deck of the Browns' beach house. From late afternoon to evening.

Act Two

The deck of Camilla's beach house. The following morning.

Act Three

The deck of the Browns' beach house. That evening.

ACT ONE

NOTE: *Throughout, there is the stage direction "Front," meaning, of course, that the character looks at and speaks directly to the audience. There is, however, no change in tone or position; and any other characters present, their hearing being intact, hear everything that is said and react accordingly.*

ACT ONE

Scene: The deck of the BROWNS' *beach house. The end of a lovely summer afternoon.*

The deck (which is new and dotted with modern beach furniture) has a slightly odd look inasmuch as it was tacked on to an old, rambling Gothic farmhouse recently moved to these dunes overlooking the beach. There are shuttered windows and screened doors on the house; a veranda; and around to one side, a main entrance from the path leading to the road in back. The deck sweeps across the stage and as far front as possible, broken there by a small flight of steps leading down to the dune and, if one continues off left, to the beach below.

When the curtain rises, an exuberant, attractive, sun-tanned woman is smiling at us. She wears a faded straw hat, and a blouse and skirt of summer beach colors: CAMILLA JABLONSKI.

CAMILLA *(Front)* Hello. I'm Camilla Jablonski. I'd like to welcome you to the South Shore of Long Island. I love it here: you can breathe. Take a breath. Go on, take a big one. Don't be afraid; the air is still good here. Besides, it's summer, and who can be afraid of anything in summer? *(She takes off her hat)* This house used to be on my father's farm. Thirty-five years ago he was hoodwinked into buying a half-mile of these dunes sight unseen. He thought he was getting a kingdom of farmland, but in those days the whole kit and kaboodle of beach wasn't worth a pile of—I don't know you well enough yet. So, he hired out as a hand, and

3

scrimped and saved all over again. Still, it took me, my four brothers, and one helluva depression to get the old man his farm. By the time he died—eighty-three he was, with his hair still red and his fist still shaking—this beach was worth ten farms. Think he cared? Not two hoots and a holler in hell. A farm was what he wanted, so a farm was what he got.

But everything's changing so fast: that wonderful old man's farm is part of an air base now and I had the house moved across our local Mason-Dixon line. That's the big highway out there. North are the truck farmers and the handymen. South: the commuters, summer people—and now: us. But there she is, sitting pretty on these dunes. And there you are, sitting pretty in the ocean. Don't worry, the tide is out.

> (*The afternoon light which has been glowing around* CAMILLA *now spreads to include the farmhouse. A little boy with shrewd beady eyes, wearing a light shirt, shorts and sneakers, opens the door for a round pretty woman. Like her conventional print dress,* LILY BROWN *is girlish, flowery, and clinging. She has a treasured Southern accent. As* CAMILLA *talks,* LILY *and her son cross to a flagpole beyond the deck and* CARY *formally presents* LILY *with a toy bugle*)

CAMILLA (*Front*) Lately, I've been renting it for the summer. This year my tenant is a Mrs. Lily Brown. That's her son, Cary. They have a nutty little ceremony they like to perform at the end of every afternoon.

LILY (*To* CAMILLA) Privately.

CAMILLA O.K. I'm going. (*Puts on her hat. Front*) Oh. After thirty-five some women get poodles, I got hats.

(She goes off. LILY *begins to chant "Retreat" on her bugle while* CARY *lowers the flag. A few bars of* LILY's *humming and* CARY's *rope pulling, and the center screen door opens.* DEEDEE GROGAN, *the blue-haired woman who comes out, stares aghast. Angular and attractive,* DEEDEE *—also in her forties—wears chic slacks, spike-heeled sandals, a huge handbag, and is always smoking. The slam of the screen door behind her interrupts the ceremony for a moment.* CARY *stares until* DEEDEE, *who has ambled down from the veranda to the deck, ducks her cigarette behind her and slouches to attention. Then* CARY *works the ropes,* LILY *"bugles" until the last note floats away and the flag is quiet in the boy's hands. During the following, he folds it and goes into the house.* LILY *turns apologetically to* DEEDEE)

LILY I'm lonely for the sound of bugles.

DEEDEE *(Front)* At least, she's lonely for something she's known. *(To* LILY) Do you have a favorite chair?

LILY *(Eagerly)* As it happens—

DEEDEE Sit in it. I have something unpleasant to discuss.

LILY Why, Mrs. Grogan! What could *you* ever discuss that could *possibly* be unpleasant?!

DEEDEE The invisible bride-to-be.

LILY Oh.
    (She sits)

5

DEEDEE (*Front*) Mr. Grogan and I arrived here from Alaska hours ago. It's off-season there and always will be. And I loathe suspense. All kinds. The worst is wondering just when your children are going to stop loving you. That's why I only had two. (*To* LILY) Does your daughter still love you? Oh, you'd answer yes anyway. But does she love my son? Why are you wriggling so?

LILY Actually—

DEEDEE You're afraid of me. (*Front*) I'm all an act! All made up. But—custom-made. (*She sits. To* LILY) I'm sure there's a simple little explanation for your daughter's absence, isn't there?

LILY How *is* Alaska?

DEEDEE A suburb of Los Angeles. And don't try to sidetrack me. (*Front*) I have a free-floating mind, so it's easily done.

LILY (*She is constantly fetching shell ash trays for* DEEDEE) I just asked because we were all so flattered that you and Mr. Grogan would travel such a great distance—(*Front*) —they have their own private airplane— (*To* DEEDEE) —and on such short notice. I mean with the wedding being set for this Sunday and all. I told Schuyler you would want to make more than the mere acquaintance of his future bride and her family. But you know how impatient young people are. (*Front*) Though I always think it's the middle-aged who ought to hurry. (*To* DEEDEE) Don't you?

DEEDEE (*Stares at her, then front*) Well—it's her house.

6

LILY Oh no. It's a summer rental. A peculiar woman owns it by the name of—

DEEDEE Mrs. Brown, you *are* trying to sidetrack me.

LILY Heavens, no! You sidetracked me.

DEEDEE I did?

LILY Yes, honey. You asked me first off if I had a favorite chair but you never let me answer. Well, I *do!* This rocker: we toted it to every Post where the General was in command. Oh, I know the glory of being the wife of a Post Commander can't seem very glorious to a woman in *your* position—

DEEDEE My dear girl, I come from simple New England fisher folk. From a long long line of fisher folk, I grant you. But people of very few words—something apparently unheard of in your part of the country. Now sit down, take a deep breath and before it runs out, answer me: where is your daughter?

LILY (*Sits in rocker*) Norma?
      (CARY *comes out*)

DEEDEE I thought you had only one daughter.

LILY Yes but I have two sons. Clark—now he's sixteen and upstairs with the mumps. He's planning to enter the ministry.

7

DEEDEE Mumps at sixteen? (*Front*) He might better plan to enter the priesthood.

LILY Cary—come here, honey—is ten. (*As he comes over*) And Norma—

DEEDEE Yes: *Norma.*

LILY —is twenty-two. They are each six years apart.

DEEDEE (*Flicking ashes into the shell* LILY *holds for her*) You seem to have a passion for neatness.

LILY Cary is going to be a General like his daddy was. Aren't you, lamb?

CARY No. I'm going to be a *nuclear* general.

LILY (*Proudly*) He can explain just what to do when the bomb falls. Would you like to—

CARY When the bomb falls—

DEEDEE Later, dear boy.
(CARY *bangs his drum, executes a sharp military turn, and goes in*)

LILY Cary goes to military school.

DEEDEE (*Front*) Both my children, of course, went to progressive school. Now then, my dear Mrs. Brown—

8

LILY (*Starting in*) —Now Clark on the other hand—

DEEDEE Mrs. Brown—

LILY Surely you want to meet the whole family—

DEEDEE (*Rises*) ROSE!

LILY Rose?

DEEDEE That *is* your name.

LILY No. It's Lily.

DEEDEE Oh. Well, I'm impossible on names. (*Front*) Lily. And you must call me Deedee.

LILY Deedee.

DEEDEE It's the bride I want—

LILY I have a sister named Rose. And one named Hyacinth. Momma wanted everyone to call us the Flower Girls . . . but no one ever did. (DEEDEE *advances on her*) Now, I named *my* children for my favorite screen stars. Norma for Norma Shearer, Clark for Clark Gable and Cary for—
    (DEEDEE *pushes her down into a chair*)

DEEDEE What is wrong with your daughter?

9

LILY What about a drink? Please. It's easier to talk through a drink.

DEEDEE A glass of champagne.

LILY Thank you! (*Gets up happily, then turns back*) Oh, I *am* sorry. There's just tons for the reception. I should have thought to chill a bottle or two but—

DEEDEE Whatever you're having will do.
    (*The following goes very fast.* LILY *continuously steps to and away from the liquor wagon on the porch*)

LILY Sherry?

DEEDEE Fine.

LILY Or would you prefer Scotch? No, a martini!

DEEDEE It doesn't matter.

LILY I'd love to mix a martini for you—

DEEDEE Don't bother to make one just for me—

LILY I'll have one with you!

DEEDEE Not if you don't really want to—

LILY Oh I do! If you do.

DEEDEE I do.

LILY   Good! Or would you prefer Scotch?

CARY   (*Comes out; indicating* DEEDEE) Mother, her maid wants to see her.
(*He bangs his drum and exits*)

DEEDEE   Mrs. Brown, what did you and the General drink every evening after the flag was lowered so gloriously?

LILY   Bourbon old-fashioned.

DEEDEE   Then for God's sake, let's have bourbon old-fashioneds and be done with it!
(*She slams into the house.* LILY *starts to mix the drinks as a good-looking young man comes striding onto the deck from around the house:* SCHUYLER GROGAN. *He wears the correct sports shirt, slacks and shoes*)

SCHUYLER   Where's Norma?

LILY   Why, Schuyler! I thought you were with your father!

SCHUYLER   I managed to leave him at the club.

LILY   The Southampton Club, I hope. A man like Tucker Grogan—

SCHUYLER   Mrs. Brown, is Norma asleep again?

LILY   Of course not! She's—trying on her wedding dress. It came from New York this morning and it didn't fit *quite* right. Well, *there* she was, the ceremony just *three* days away and—

SCHUYLER You're spilling everything.
(*He takes over the bartending*)

LILY I should have known to have champagne for your mother: a woman who brings her own maid wherever she goes! (*Front*) And a maid who complains about her room! (*To* SCHUYLER) I hope after you and Norma are married, Norma will have a maid of her own, too.

SCHUYLER Is that why you want her to marry me?

LILY Schuyler, many bachelors passed through my little home town. But the only eligible was Captain Bert Brown and Momma chose him for me. At the time, of course, Momma did not know he had come up through the ranks.

SCHUYLER When Norma and I are married—

LILY Yes, dear—

SCHUYLER (*Front*) —Norma is going to have a cleaning woman, not a personal maid. She is going to have a martini before dinner, not champagne. She is going to be called Mother by our children, not Norma, Normie, NooNoo, NahNah, NeeNee, NiyNiy, but *Mother*. I'm a young lawyer, starting out, with a small, solid firm that has no connections with any of my father's or grandfather's corporations. I intend to live on that—and so will Norma, after we're married.

LILY Of course she will, honey. She loves you. She told me the exact moment she realized it. Last winter, not long after you began going steady, you took her to the movies one night, and right in the middle, she heard a funny little noise —and there you were: crying!

SCHUYLER I haven't cried since my mother visited me in prep school. (*He turns, for* DEEDEE *has come out again*) Hello, Mother.

DEEDEE Deedee.

SCHUYLER Audrey, if you must.

DEEDEE That is not my name.

SCHUYLER It's the name you were born with.

DEEDEE (*Sitting in chair*) I cannot have my own son call me Audrey.

SCHUYLER I cannot call my own mother Deedee.

DEEDEE Then don't call me, I'll call you. (*He starts in*) Schuyler! If you're looking for your fiancée, she's upstairs trying on her wedding gown.

LILY (*Going to* DEEDEE) She is??

SCHUYLER Have you seen her?

DEEDEE No. (*Taking drink from* LILY) Elisabet told me. (*Front*) Elisabet is my maid. Much happier in her new room. (*To* SCHUYLER) What made you cry in prep school?

SCHUYLER Why can't you leave the eavesdropping to Elisabet?

DEEDEE But I do! (*Front*) She also peeps through keyholes. I suppose it's unfair to bring her into someone else's home, and I should sack her—but: she's an atheist.

LILY Are you?

DEEDEE I'm much too social. But she's brilliant with my hair, and who else would hire a maid who doesn't even fear God? (*To* SCHUYLER) Did you know your fiancée has been in this house the whole afternoon? (*To* LILY) Why haven't you wanted me to see her?

LILY Well—

DEEDEE With the haste of this marriage, I'd say she was pregnant—but I know my son.

SCHUYLER There was nothing hasty about the marriage. It was planned in the spring.

DEEDEE . . . In the spring.
    (*A moment*)

LILY Such a lovely season!

SCHUYLER   You and Father were in Majorca.

DEEDEE   We went by air, Schuyler, like letters. (*Rising*) And for our summer holiday in Alaska, we went air mail too, like your tardy wedding invitation. Ah! . . . You didn't mean for us to accept.

SCHUYLER   Of course I did.

LILY   It was just that he was so impatient! He wouldn't even wait for his own sister to get here!

DEEDEE   I wouldn't expect him to.

SCHUYLER   I explained there wouldn't be time, since Nina lives in Paris.

DEEDEE   (*Front*)   With a French woman who has very short hair and writes very long novels.

SCHUYLER   Mother—!

DEEDEE   (*Front*)   Naturally, we don't speak to her.

LILY   Why not?

SCHUYLER   Because we don't speak French! (*Then, to* DEEDEE) You always do this!

DEEDEE   And you judge me only by the way I look! You thought I'd try to break up this misalliance. That's why you didn't tell me about it until my hands were tied!

15

SCHUYLER That is not—

DEEDEE But it was fine to tell Daisy!

SCHUYLER Who?

DEEDEE Daisy! Her!

SCHUYLER We didn't tell her until last month.

LILY And then just so's I'd have time to arrange for the ceremony.
　　(*A moment*)

SCHUYLER (*Front*) My mother would've turned my wedding into a fancy dress carnival for her friends. That's the reason I didn't want her to know sooner. (*To* DEEDEE) And that's the only reason. I've planned a small wedding in a small church and I would like for my mother and father to give me their blessing.

DEEDEE (*Quietly, after a moment*) We're here, Schuyler. We're ready with our blessing. And I didn't like coming back here. (*Front*) I was pregnant with his sister along this very same stretch of sea. I hate the sea: it never listens and it's always interrupting. (*To* SCHUYLER) My God, what a time that was! I was too grotesque to do anything but swelter on a screened porch and look down on the beach through binoculars. (*Suddenly, to* LILY) What did you say her name was?

LILY Who?

DEEDEE That woman you rent this wandering house from.

LILY I didn't say.

DEEDEE Well, do say.

LILY Jablonski.

DEEDEE Jablonski.

LILY (*Going to her*) Such an un*musical* name, really.

DEEDEE Her first name isn't Camilla?

LILY Yes! Isn't it awful!

DEEDEE (*Laughs; then front*) This house is cursed. (*Descending beach steps*) It didn't used to be on these dunes at all. It was a farmhouse; it's been moved here. Yes! This deck has been added on. This is the house of Camilla Jablonski all right and I put a curse on it myself, that swollen summer!

SCHUYLER What did she ever do to you?

DEEDEE Nothing! (*To* SCHUYLER *as she mounts steps to the deck*) I never actually met the Jablonski. I merely saw her through binoculars. Why don't you invite her to the wedding?

LILY Oh, honey, Mrs. Jablonski is definitely not a type to invite to a wedding of substance!

DEEDEE Mrs? *Mrs.* Jablonski?

LILY Yes.

DEEDEE Someone married her?

LILY She has a grown son who rides along the beach on an overdressed horse.

DEEDEE She wasn't married that summer.

SCHUYLER Then she isn't the woman you're talking about. This one's name wouldn't have been *Miss* Camilla Jablonski.

DEEDEE Two creatures with that name? Impossible! (*Sitting in a chair*) How old is yours?

LILY My what?

DEEDEE Your Camilla Jablonski.

LILY I'm perfectly impossible on age. I never know—

DEEDEE Roughly, darling, roughly.

LILY She's about our age.

DEEDEE (*Coldly*) Really. Well, my intuition tells me it's the same creature and this is the same house. (*Front*) Which means large trouble for someone.
　　(*The door opens, and out comes* NORMA BROWN, *a pretty girl in her early twenties, wearing a floating white wed-*

ding dress in the style of a medieval princess, with a veil over her head, and very high heels)

SCHUYLER Norma!

LILY Honey, you look like a princess out of a fairy story.

SCHUYLER (*Leads her down a step, takes off her veil. Front*)
Now. Do you wonder that I'm in love with her?

LILY (*Front*) It's bad luck for him to be seeing her in her wedding dress.
(NORMA *shows her ring out front, and takes veil from* SCHUYLER)

DEEDEE Primitive superstition.

NORMA (*A dazzling smile, and she goes to* DEEDEE *and extends her hand*) You must be Mother Grogan.

DEEDEE (*Withdraws her hand; accusingly to* SCHUYLER) You told her to call me that!

NORMA If it's wrong, I apologize. And for not greeting you when you arrived. But you see, I was—I was—

DEEDEE Yes?

NORMA (*Desperately*) I was—

SCHUYLER Having her dress fixed for the wedding.

NORMA Yes! Having my dress fixed for the wedding.
(*Yawns*)

LILY Norma!

NORMA Yes? (*Then, alarmed*) Oh, Momma! Schuyler, I'm
sorry. Was I—?

SCHUYLER Not quite.

LILY You'd better go up.

DEEDEE She's just come down. (*To* NORMA) Not quite what?
(SCHUYLER *seats* NORMA *in rocker*)

NORMA (*Charm again*) Not quite—ah—ready to greet you
when you arrived. Please forgive me.

DEEDEE I already have.

NORMA Thank you. How was your trip?

DEEDEE Smooth.

NORMA I'm so glad. (*Starts to yawn,* SCHUYLER *shakes the
rocker*) How is—ah—Mr. Grogan? I'm longing to meet
him.
(*But the yawn erupts in the middle of this and her eyes
start to close*)

SCHUYLER Norma, would you like a drink?

LILY (*Going to* NORMA) Schuyler, get her one!
(*He goes to the bar, hands drink to* LILY, *who hands it to* NORMA *as:*)

NORMA A drink? My how time flies!

DEEDEE What?

NORMA It must be seven.

DEEDEE It isn't even six.

NORMA Then I can't have a drink.
(*Returns the drink*)

DEEDEE Why not?

NORMA (*Front*) We have martinis at seven. Dinner at eight, breakfast at nine, beach at ten, lunch at one. (*Starting to slow down*) Tennis at three; tea at five; drinks at seven.
(*Yawns*)

LILY (*Furtively patting her*) Norma . . . Norma! . . .

NORMA (*Brightly*) Dinner at eight; bridge at ten; bed at one; breakfast at nine; tennis at three; lunch at one . . . martinis at . . .
(*And she falls back asleep*)

LILY Norma? . . . NORMA! (*She throws the veil over* NORMA's *face. The bang of the drum, and* CARY *is back*) Oh, Cary, not now!
(*Ducks under the veil*)

CARY I have an important communiqué.

LILY Later. Norma?

DEEDEE It's very bad to frustrate a child. What is it, dear boy?

CARY The downstairs Uh-Uh is stopped up.

LILY I've already called Mrs. Jablonski. Norma . . .

DEEDEE (*To* CARY) If by Uh-Uh you mean "toilet," say so. Otherwise, you're going to grow up a mass of nasty inhibitions.
(LILY *and* SCHUYLER *huddle in a conference*)

CARY Yes, ma'am.

DEEDEE Now say it. Toilet.

CARY (*Very low*) Toilet.

DEEDEE *Toilet.*

CARY Toilet. *Toilet.* (*Banging the drum in rhythm*) TOILET, TOILET—
(*At this* NORMA, *her eyes still closed, suddenly rises and starts to follow* CARY *who is shouting and drumming as he exits*)

DEEDEE (*Rises*) Where's she going?

LILY (*Guiding* NORMA *toward the house*) Upstairs to change!

DEEDEE Nonsense. I want to talk to her.
(*Guides* NORMA *back*)

LILY Schuyler, where's that drink?

DEEDEE She can't. It isn't seven.

NORMA (*Eyes open, she smiles*) No. Drinks are at seven.
Dinner's at eight; bridge at ten. (*Yawns and sinks onto the
beach mat at the top of the steps*) Bed at one . . . breakfast
at nine . . . beach at . . .

DEEDEE There she goes again! (*And* NORMA *is asleep again
on the mat. They all stare at her*) How long has this been
going on?

LILY The first time I saw it was at a Junior League Tea.
But that was just a cat nap.

SCHUYLER Well, Saturday night, I took her to a dance at the
club, and that was no cat nap. (*Front*) She was asleep the
entire time we were on the dance floor. And she was cut in
on five times!

DEEDEE I had no idea she was such an accomplished dancer!

LILY (*Front*) My daughter has all the social graces.

SCHUYLER Physically, she's perfect.

DEEDEE A virgin?

SCHUYLER Mother!
   (*He walks away*)

DEEDEE Well, she *is* twenty-two. But assuming she is a virgin, it's quite simple. The dear girl is petrified of her wedding night. An elementary Freudian escape. Take her to an analyst.

LILY She's been.

DEEDEE She has?!

LILY When she was eighteen.

DEEDEE (*Front*) Both my children were analyzed before and during puberty.

LILY At that time, she was always tearing up calendars.

DEEDEE Calendars?

LILY So I took her to the Post psychiatrist.

DEEDEE An Army man? That's hardly being analyzed.

LILY Well, it took years and she didn't sit up once! She'd probably still be lying there if they hadn't made the General retire. But when he did, we moved into the city and Norma began watching television again. And by the time Schuyler met her—

SCHUYLER (*Front*) She seemed exactly what I wanted.

24

LILY   But, honey, she is!

DEEDEE   (*Front*) My son has finally surprised me! Do you know what I expected to find as the bride of his choice? A beige girl: beige hair, beige eyes, beige personality. This girl is an original! I shall be proud to have her as my daughter-in-law.

LILY   Bravo!

SCHUYLER   Bravo my butt! (*Front; indicating* LILY) Excuse me, but all she wants is a good marriage for her daughter. And all my mother wants is a conversation piece for her son!

DEEDEE   (*Front*) I want someone who will be a challenge to him. What do *you* want?

SCHUYLER   I want her to wake up.

DEEDEE   Do you? Well, that all depends on why she's sleeping. (*Pausing at door*) You know, the reason might very easily be you, Schuyler. (*Opens the door*) Or you, Violet. (*And goes in*)

LILY   I think the reason is this house. But I rented it from that peculiar Jablonski woman because with the General gone, I just had to be close to the last post we knew. (*The light is dusking; she sits by* NORMA) Where the people and the shapes and the sounds were familiar. But the people have moved on and the shapes are strange and the sounds are a little frightening. Sometimes, when the wind is right, you can almost hear the bugles. Blowing at the same time for the same events. As long as you are within the sound of those bugles, you are safe. . . . We couldn't hear them in the city. And day by day, the General got tireder and quieter. Until one day, he was just quiet forever. (*She gets up*) Schuyler, that isn't what's happening to Norma, is it?

SCHUYLER No, it's probably just being back near the Post.

LILY Yes, of course. That's it. (*Going to the house*) And this house. (*Front*) A house keeps the character of its owner, and that awful Mrs. Jablonski is a very unsettling woman!
> (*She goes in.* SCHUYLER *hesitates, then sits by* NORMA *and speaks very softly as he lifts the veil* LILY *has covered her with*)

SCHUYLER Norma? . . . Why do you sleep? Is it because of me? You're everything I want as my wife. Everything except the sleeping. Every night, I want so much to take you to bed. Sometimes, even during the day. But I control myself. Can't you control yourself? (*Bends over her*) Can't you wake up and stay awake? Wake up, please!
> (*He looks up to see* CARY *eavesdropping. Then:*)

CARY Shhhh!
> (*He continues to watch as* SCHUYLER *replaces the veil*)

SCHUYLER (*Front*) Why? Why does she sleep?
> (*Chased by* CARY's *baleful look, he goes into the house. Satisfied,* CARY *goes in, too. The light begins to form a rose-colored pool around* NORMA. *The wash of the waves*

gets louder; then over it, approaching hoof beats on the sand. The horse stops, and there is whistling from off, and a young man comes on. AARON *is 20: healthy, open good looks. His faded pants are crowded down into old boots; on his head, a worn felt hat with a small feather; a plumber's plunger for cleaning drains and a tool kit in his hands; a sunny, cocky manner. When he sees* NORMA, *he stops whistling and stares as he mounts the steps by her and walks past. Suddenly, there is the sweet sound of a violin; he stops dead. A moment—then he sets his pole and tool kit down against the veranda rail, walks back to* NORMA *and sits on his heels by her. He looks at her a moment, then gently leans down and lets his lips touch hers. Nothing. He sits up, frowning, then down again and really kisses her. He breaks and starts up, but though her eyes remain closed, her head moves up and her lips press out for more. He obliges. Then they break and her eyes open and they look deeply at each other*)

NORMA Are you a prince?

AARON (*Grins*) Sure.

NORMA I knew it.

AARON How?

NORMA Why else would you kiss me with your hat on?

AARON How many years have you been asleep?

NORMA Have I been asleep again?

AARON Don't you know??

NORMA It happens so often lately. (*Front*) There I am, listening hard as I can to people. And then—conversation becomes a noise of voices. I make my noise like everybody else: "Yes, that certainly is right. Oh, I couldn't agree more." It always fits, even without listening. And then—my eyelids seem to drop shut— (*They do*) —for the smallest moment. But when I open them— (*She does*) —it can be an hour later, even a day later—but the noise of voices is exactly the same. And when I make my noise, it fits right in! So you see, I never can tell whether I've been asleep or not. For all I know, they've been asleep too!

AARON They probably have. But with their eyes open.

NORMA I wish I could manage that.

AARON No, you don't.

NORMA Yes, I do. They think I'm peculiar.

AARON Tell 'em they're peculiar.

NORMA But they're not! I'm the only one who sleeps with my eyes shut. They all sleep with their eyes open.

AARON (*Laughing*) Then who's peculiar?

NORMA (*Thinks for a moment*) You are.
        (*Lies back. Her eyes shut and stay shut during:*)

28

AARON You won't fall asleep on me.

NORMA You're so very sure.

AARON Yes.
      (*He leans down to kiss her*)

NORMA No.

AARON Why not?

NORMA I'm to be married in three days.

AARON That's all right.

NORMA (*Bolts upright, eyes now open*) That's all right?!?

AARON I don't want to marry you, I want to make love with you.

NORMA (*Standing now on steps below him*) You're no prince!

AARON I've got a castle.

NORMA Sand!

AARON *On* sand, the summer one. It's right down the beach: modern and very glassy. But the winter one—I know you'd like. Lots of turrets and bay windows. In fact, the winter castle— (*He gestures toward the house*) —is here.

NORMA   Here?!?

AARON   It's yours for the summer.

NORMA   Who are you?

AARON   A prince, as you said. The Prince Jablonski, given
name of—
       (*He jumps off the deck—tips his hat*)

NORMA   Aaron Jablonski and you are *here to fix the plumbing!*

AARON   Well, since I'm your landlord—

NORMA   You're a plumber! (*Descending the steps angrily*)
And if you're anything like the other boys around— (*Next
to him now, she stops and stares*) —why, you're *smaller*
than I am!

AARON   Shorter, not smaller. And without those heels—

NORMA   How old are you? I think you're also *younger* than
I am!

AARON   (*Front*)   What a silly little girl.

NORMA   (*Front*)   I happen to be twenty-two!

AARON   (*Front*)   I'm fifty years older than she is and I was
twenty on my last birthday.

NORMA   You *are* younger than I am!

AARON Oh, and poorer than you are; and socially lower than you are. Did you go to college?

NORMA Over two years. Did you?

AARON Less than two years. Why didn't you finish?

NORMA Girls don't finish. Why didn't you?

AARON They only teach what's in the books. O.K., what else: Are you a virgin?

NORMA I won't answer that!

AARON You don't have to. I'm less pure and more corrupt than you are. All in all, completely beneath you.

NORMA I'm glad you realize it.
  (*She starts to go in*)

AARON (*Stops her*) Were you thinking of me as a husband?

NORMA Of course not!

AARON Then why check my qualifications?

NORMA I'm a girl: it's habit.

AARON But you're to be married in three days.

NORMA Oh, take your hat off; no, put it back on; no, take it off. Oh, I don't care what you do with it!

AARON Don't you?

NORMA (*Music begins*) You upset me. The man I am going to marry makes me feel safe. And comes from a fine family.

AARON My father met my mother while she was dozing in the sun just like you were.

NORMA He's everything you're not—including a gentleman!

AARON Well, *you* upset *me*—and I don't like it.

NORMA . . . You'd better go fix the plumbing right now.

AARON After all this, I couldn't. It'd offend my sense of style.

NORMA Then go back to your summer castle—and stay there.

AARON And what will you do?

NORMA I'll go ahead with my wedding as though nothing happened. Because, plumber, nothing did.

AARON Everything did, and nothing's the same. (*She turns to go*) Turn your back: that proves it. (*She takes a few steps*) Run away: that proves it more. (*She turns to glare at him*) Look at me: that proves it most . . . I don't want a wife, but I want you.

NORMA Well, I don't want you. I *am* going to be married and if you will excuse me, I have to take a nap before dinner.
(*She starts into the house*)

AARON (*Grinning as he calls out:*) I'll bet you can't!
(*She shoots him a look and storms into the house as, whistling the melody of the violin, he picks up his plumber's pole and cheerfully goes down the steps. The music continues, the sky deepens to blue evening, and the lights in the house begin to come on.* CARY *comes out to pick up a chair: it is too heavy. He goes to the bar, takes a good whiff of a bottle of whiskey, coughs, puts the bottle back, and picks up the chair as though it were light as a feather, and takes it into the house. He returns and sees the plumber's kit which* AARON *has left behind.* CARY *starts to steal it—but the music changes, and* CAMILLA *comes up the ramp onto the deck. The boy runs into the house.* CAMILLA *goes to the house and, with love, leans against a pole. A board is loose: she opens the kit, takes out a hammer and whams the board into place as* NORMA *comes out the center door in a dinner dress. She is upset, unaware that she is tearing a large sheet of paper to pieces*)

CAMILLA Look at that evening: Goddam nature! (*Takes off her hat, saluting the sky*) Many thanks. (*To* NORMA) That's to my father—I hope. He used to say: "Camilla, fifty percent of the secret of happiness is knowing what you want." Sounds easy. But do you know what you want?

NORMA I think so.

CAMILLA Then what're you tearing up there?

NORMA Only the page off a calendar— Oh, Lord!

33

CAMILLA Relax: that's not so terrible.

NORMA (*Front*) Not to her family. (*To* CAMILLA) I suppose you've heard I'm peculiar.

CAMILLA No. Are you?

NORMA Don't you think so?

CAMILLA Just because you're a little different, that doesn't mean you're peculiar.

NORMA You sound just like Aaron.

CAMILLA Ohh, *you're* the Sleeping Beauty!

NORMA You knew that.

CAMILLA No.

NORMA Why else did you come by?

CAMILLA I love this old house and I get to missing it. So every now and then, while you're all at supper, I come by to say Hello, touch it, and say Goodbye till fall.

NORMA (*Front*) If she were my mother, I might not believe her. But she's his mother. (*To* CAMILLA) You are, all right. He certainly knows what *he* wants!
　　(*She starts fussing with the pieces of paper again*)

CAMILLA I hope so.
　　(*Gently takes the pieces*)

Jane Fonda and Celeste Holm, as
NORMA and CAMILLA

NORMA Mrs. Jablonski . . . what's the other fifty percent?

CAMILLA *Doing* what you really want. (*She throws the pieces of paper into the moonlight at the side of the deck. Magically, they shimmer and rock back and forth, floating to the ground like petal blossoms.* CAMILLA *turns front with a grin*) Anybody can do it.

NORMA How?

CAMILLA Just try, sweetheart. And call me Camilla. Everybody does except summer people.

NORMA But I'm summer people.

CAMILLA No. They only live a few weeks out of the year. No, not you: falling asleep, tearing calendars—

NORMA Look at me.

CAMILLA . . . Well, you don't have to be if you don't want to be.

NORMA You're a very upsetting family.
(*Bright, white deck lights go on and* LILY *calls from inside:*)

LILY Ooh-ooh! Ooh-ooh! (*Comes out with brandy*) I have your brandy—Norma, what are you doing out here? (CAMILLA *hands some of the pieces of paper to* NORMA) You upset everyone at the dinner table, leave your fiancé sitting like a bachelor. Mrs. Jablonski, this is no time to fix the drains.

CAMILLA (*Getting tool kit and starting off*) My son'll be over first thing in the morning.
(NORMA *looks at her, goes in and closes the door*)

LILY Early, I hope. Good night.

CAMILLA Good night.

LILY Ooh-ooh! Mr. Grogan, Mr. Grogan!

CAMILLA Mrs. Brown, excuse me. That Mr. Grogan.

LILY Is *the* Mr. Tucker Grogan, yes! He and Mrs. Tucker Grogan are staying here, guests in my house! Well, your house, but my guests. Isn't that miraculous?
(*Rolls up the deck mat and places it on the porch*)

CAMILLA It really is. (*Front*) Some names you've known so long, you think you know the people attached to them. And some people you haven't known for so long, you think they're only names. Then suddenly, you realize they're not; and you get afraid. Or excited. Or afraid to be excited.

LILY (*Front*) What on God's green earth is that woman talking about?
(*She goes in*)

CAMILLA I'm talking about someone I thought I'd never know again. You take life as it comes, and sometimes you get a lovely surprise!
(*There is music: a handsome gray-haired man in dinner clothes has entered behind her:* TUCKER GROGAN. *A pause as he comes down and they look at each other*)

36

TUCKER All evening, this house has been whispering to me. This afternoon, in the sunlight, it was quiet and polite—as though we'd just met. But right before dinner, when the sun went down, I looked at that porch and the whispering began. You had it moved here, didn't you? (*She nods*) And the swing was over there. (*Again she nods*) I always thought if we ever met again, it would be either on the porch or the beach. Now it's both.

CAMILLA I always thought it would be at the opera.

TUCKER Since when do you go to the opera?

CAMILLA I don't.

TUCKER Neither do I.

CAMILLA I know.
          (*They laugh*)

TUCKER Why do you look so young?

CAMILLA Everyone looks young in the summer.

TUCKER But why are you even more attractive?

CAMILLA I'm happy. You're pretty attractive yourself, Tucker. Are you happy?

TUCKER I'm rich.

CAMILLA I read about you in the papers. Such big deals!

37

TUCKER   Money makes money.

CAMILLA   I was in the papers once myself. My house was robbed. Not this one. A new one, down the beach. Very modern. We drew our own plans and built it ourselves.

TUCKER   We?

CAMILLA   (*Evasively*)   The builder and I. A local type.

TUCKER   Not your husband.

CAMILLA   No.

TUCKER   You're not married.

CAMILLA   Not at the moment. Good night.
(*She descends the steps*)

TUCKER   (*Following*)   Where are you going?

CAMILLA   You make me nervous. It's so sudden after all these years. You look like Tucker and you don't look like Tucker.

TUCKER   I haven't changed that much.

CAMILLA   It's too soon to tell. I've got two or three hundred years in my eyes and this lousy plumber's kit in my hand. Tucker, I'm very glad to see you.

TUCKER   I'm very glad to see you, Camilla. And the hell with being nervous.

CAMILLA The hell with it . . . Was I special to you? (*Front*) What a dumb thing to ask! What can he say but yes?

TUCKER You're the reason I love summer.

CAMILLA (*Front*) That's pretty nice, huh? (*To him*) Well, you're the reason I'm attractive.

TUCKER That's very nice (*Front*) but not true.

CAMILLA It is. And it's funny how easy it is to say it now.

TUCKER How did I make you attractive?

CAMILLA By wanting me. Until that summer we met, I was one of those girls, men don't think of as girls. They tell you their troubles, then ask you to fix them up with your best friend. Even when I went to kid parties and played Post Office, I never got a Special Delivery. And when I graduated high school, two of my brothers had to take me to the prom to make sure I'd be cut in on.

TUCKER Come on, you were a very pretty girl.

CAMILLA Yes, but I just wasn't attractive: I didn't look like I had a secret. (*Front*) I was scared, and believe me, nobody is more scared than a female who thinks she's going to die without ever knowing what an old maid never knows. And then—then it was as though one night, I was standing on the porch of that house wishing on a star, and on the beach, the very next morning, was the wish and the star to boot. And he wanted me.

TUCKER Very much.

CAMILLA (*Front*) He always was polite.

TUCKER No. I mean it.

LILY (*Off*) Ooh-ooh, Mr. Grogan!

TUCKER Where is that new house of yours?

CAMILLA Next one down the beach.

TUCKER I'll be over to see it tomorrow.

CAMILLA I'll wash my hair.
(*She goes.* TUCKER *jumps happily up on the deck as* LILY *comes out the upper door with his brandy*)

LILY How did you get out here? I have been searching every nook and cranny of these premises for you!

TUCKER Mrs. Brown, I go to so many houses and each time I think: this time I'll find a lovely surprise. (*In his happiness he puts his arm around her*) But this time, oh, this time, I really have—

LILY (*Overlapping*) Mr. Grogan, I am no surprise! I am the mother of three, including your son's fiancée—
(*As she is protesting,* DEEDEE *comes out. She wears sleek dinner pajamas, carries a glass of champagne and is smoking a small cigar. There is an awkward pause as*

she slowly walks by them, sits, raises her glass to them and drinks)

LILY You are jumping to false conclusions. You are not being fair!

DEEDEE To be fair is to be frustrated. Now let's all have a drink. You're a good-hearted woman, Iris, and I'm quite fond of you.

LILY May I say something? My name is not Iris. And I never had to worry about the General. Never.
(She goes and sits in the rocker)

DEEDEE I myself come from a long long line of fisher folk and I never worry about anything. Including Tucker. Because I am never fooled. Not ever.

TUCKER *(Front)* Well, hardly ever.
(SCHUYLER comes out, correct in his dinner clothes and happy. He carries a backgammon case)

LILY Where's Norma?

SCHUYLER She went upstairs to bed.

DEEDEE Oh, why? She was superb at dinner! All that gabble about princes and castles! I can't wait to hear what's she going to come out with tomorrow!

SCHUYLER Tomorrow is all planned. In the morning, we rehearse at the church. I know it's summer, but— *(To TUCKER)* you will kindly wear trousers— (*To* DEEDEE) —you will kindly not.

(*He and* TUCKER *start to play backgammon*)

CARY (*Comes out in pajamas*) Mother, Clark wants to go to sleep. But the German lady keeps asking questions.

(DEEDEE *crosses into the house as:*)

LILY You should be in your own room and asleep.

CARY I *was* in my own room.

DEEDEE (*Off*) Elisabet! *Höre auf zu arbeiten und gehe schlafen!*

LILY Cary lamb, how many times has Mother told you eavesdropping is not polite?

CARY The German lady does it.

LILY That's her job. Now come on: beddy-bye.

CARY (*Indicating* DEEDEE *who has returned*) I thought you wanted me to explain to her about the bomb.

DEEDEE I thought you were joking.

CARY That is no subject for joking.

DEEDEE Then I advise you to take it more seriously.

LILY Why, he's only a child—

42

DEEDEE There are no children any more. He is a small person. And I'm sure he prefers that I converse with him as such. Don't you, dear boy?

CARY Mama, they still haven't fixed the downstairs— (*Defiantly, to* DEEDEE) —Uh-Uh.
(*He marches in*)

LILY (*Following him*) Well, I'll call Mrs. Jablonski again.

TUCKER Did you say—*Mrs.* Jablonski?

LILY The woman I rent this house from.
(*She goes in*)

DEEDEE And her first name is Camilla.
(*A pause*)

TUCKER (*Starts in*) Schuyler, I left my cigars inside.

DEEDEE Have one of mine.

SCHUYLER (*Wearily*) How long ago was it, Dad?

TUCKER Oh, years—

DEEDEE But she was the first! And she set the old boy itching. (*Front*) Oh no, not that way. (*To* SCHUYLER) No, she caused him to break out in a great rash of discontent with the life your grandfather bought for him. With your grandmother's money.

TUCKER (*Front*) While you're untangling the financial hier-
archy, let me say one thing: *she* wanted the rich life. Not I.
Laugh, but I always wanted to run a cattle ranch.

DEEDEE (*Gets up*) That was the Jablonski's idea. Until you
met her, you never *had* an idea! (SCHUYLER *starts to the
house*) But the moment he met her, I knew it. Because
suddenly I felt that to be pregnant was to be ugly.
(SCHUYLER *stops*)

TUCKER (*Front*) She says that deliberately in front of the
boy.

DEEDEE It's quite enough to have lost Nina.

TUCKER You came out here that summer to hide because *you*
thought it was ugly to be pregnant.

SCHUYLER Dad—

DEEDEE And it was *you* who did the hiding—with the Jablonski!

SCHUYLER Mother—

TUCKER (*Overlapping*) I was not hiding!

SCHUYLER It was nothing!

DEEDEE Because *I saw to it!* Through the years, I've learned
to see to it. I've even invited them into the house to get

them out of it! Why don't you ever make a pass at someone you *can't* get?

SCHUYLER Oh, I give up!

TUCKER So do I.

DEEDEE (*Front*) If only he would. (*A moment; they look at each other. Front*) Well, first thing tomorrow, he'll be padding down the beach in search of La Jablonski. I want a complete report by lunch time.

SCHUYLER I wonder if you'd be disappointed if he didn't go.

DEEDEE I'm simply as curious as he is. Do you know how he met the lady?

SCHUYLER No, and I don't want to.

DEEDEE (*Sitting*) She was the farmer's daughter—literally. She delivered vegetables to our back door, and your daddy pinched her behind across a bushel of Long Island potatoes.

TUCKER Do I have to say that is *not* how I met her?

DEEDEE Then how did you meet her?

SCHUYLER *I don't want to know!*

DEEDEE But after all these years—I do.

TUCKER I'd been fishing and I came up from the beach and there she was, lying on the dunes, dozing in the sun.
(NORMA *enters. She wears a soft blouse, slacks and low shoes*)

NORMA Who was dozing in the sun?

SCHUYLER (*Going to her*) What are you doing up?

NORMA I can't sleep!

DEEDEE (*Front*) I adore that girl!

SCHUYLER So do I. (*They kiss*) How about a drink?

NORMA A martini, please.

SCHUYLER No one has a martini after dinner.

NORMA Why not?

SCHUYLER A martini is a cocktail.

NORMA And?

SCHUYLER Cocktails are drunk before dinner.

NORMA Why?

SCHUYLER Because no one drinks them after dinner!

NORMA I do. Very dry, please.

SCHUYLER Norma—

DEEDEE Mix her the drink!

SCHUYLER Mother—

DEEDEE Call me Mother! Call me anything you want! (*Front*)
I could dance, I could waltz, I could even give up smoking
except that I like cigarettes! My son has finally paid me a
compliment. He has chosen for his bride a girl who is
exactly like me: an individual. (*Kisses* NORMA) Tucker, I'm
going to take you over at backgammon after I stand on my
head for three minutes.
   (*And the door slams after her*)

NORMA (*To* TUCKER) Mr. Grogan, you didn't marry her.

TUCKER Who?

NORMA Whoever was dozing in that sun.

TUCKER No.

SCHUYLER You wanted a martini: now drink it.
   (*She downs the drink and hands the glass back*)

NORMA Why didn't you marry her?

TUCKER I was married. (*Conscious of* SCHUYLER) Anyway,
it was nothing.

NORMA But you wanted it to be *something*.

47

SCHUYLER He didn't.

NORMA (*To* TUCKER) Why don't we just do what we want?

TUCKER Because we always have something to lose. And we're never sure it'll be worth the risk.

NORMA Why not say to hell! and risk it anyway?

TUCKER (*Front*) . . . Why not?

NORMA If we don't, we'll never know. Will we, Mr. Grogan?

TUCKER No, not ordinarily. But once in a great while, if we're very lucky, we get another chance.
(*He jauntily goes toward the house*)

NORMA Oh, that's not the same.

TUCKER Why isn't it?

NORMA We'd be too old by then. And really afraid.

TUCKER We're only too old when we can't be afraid any more.
(*He opens the door*)

SCHUYLER Are you afraid, Father?

TUCKER I'm not old, Schuyler.
(*He goes in*)

SCHUYLER May I ask why all the questions?

NORMA   There were once two princesses, and every time one opened her mouth, all that came out were pearls and rubies and emeralds. And every time the other opened her mouth, all that came out were frogs and newts and hoptoads. But then there was born a third princess and every time she opened her mouth, all that came out were questions.

SCHUYLER   You're not a princess. And I told you I didn't like women in pants.

NORMA   Your mother wears pants.

SCHUYLER   My mother. What's the opposite of an Oedipus complex? . . . Has my mother been talking at you? What happened to you just before dinner? What are you doing?

NORMA   (*She is lying on the deck as before. She stretches, deliberately*)   What does it look like I'm doing?

SCHUYLER   You're not going to sleep?

NORMA   (*Front*)   I think he wants me to.

SCHUYLER   (*Front*)   I want her to go to bed.

NORMA   With you?

SCHUYLER   The minute we're married.

NORMA   Schuyler, I had a martini *after* dinner. (*He goes to her. She reaches up, he helps her to her feet and then turns*

49

from her and walks away) Is it because you don't think it's proper? You're not a virgin.

SCHUYLER No. And it's proper for me and it's not proper for you.

NORMA (*Front*) It certainly isn't fair for me. Why half the girls I know—

SCHUYLER (*Front*) They're wrong!

NORMA Why?

SCHUYLER Because that's the way things are.

NORMA Let's change 'em.

SCHUYLER I want to go to bed with you so badly, I can't sleep. But I will not change my principles, not even to please you.

NORMA You're no prince.

SCHUYLER There are no princes any more!

NORMA *Then there should be!*
    (*Pause*)

SCHUYLER I think it's time you went upstairs.

NORMA Why?

50

SCHUYLER Listen: these questions you ask, and ones you haven't gotten around to yet—they've all been asked and answered years ago. Other answers've been tried—in my own family—but the only ones that work are the old ones, Norma. And those are the answers I have to live by.

NORMA Martinis at seven, dinner at eight, breakfast at—

SCHUYLER Yes!

NORMA I am not ready to go upstairs yet, Schuyler.
(*She sits down on the steps*)

SCHUYLER (*After a moment*) May I have my ring back?

NORMA (*A moment, then she holds her hand out to him*) Certainly!

SCHUYLER (*He comes over, looks; then:*) Where is it?

NORMA Oh!

SCHUYLER You've lost it!

NORMA It was loose and I meant to get a guard. Oh, Schuyler, I'm sorry!
(*She searches for it on all fours*)

SCHUYLER Get up. It was insured.

NORMA I'll find it and give it to you in the morning . . . If you still want it back.

SCHUYLER   If you still want to give it back. (*They look at each other, waiting*) Well—
   (*Still they wait. Then he slowly goes to the house*)

NORMA   Schuyler—

SCHUYLER   Yes?

NORMA   (*Changing her mind*)   You can turn off the lights if you will.

SCHUYLER   Sure. Good night.

NORMA   Good night (*He goes in. A moment, then the deck lights go out. She gets down on her knees as though to look for the ring, and then stretches full out, her eyes closed. From the darkness on the dunes, someone laughs, then louder. She sits up swiftly and looks out:*) Plumber? Are you out there on the dunes? Plumber? (*Again laughter. She looks in a slightly different direction*) You're no prince, Jablonski! You laugh at the wrong time and you're too sure of yourself! (*She waits: silence*) Are you still there? . . . Plumber? . . . Prince? (*The music starts*) Well, I do like your laugh. Even though you laugh at me. . . . Oh, yes you do. And don't say it's because you enjoy me: you enjoy everything. (*This catches her. Front*) He does enjoy everything, doesn't he? Why? Why is he so sure? Why is it he knows? (*She turns her face toward the dunes*) Tell me! Ah, don't go away!— Oh, no, I can't! (*Front*) I can't just wander into the night and ride away on a strange horse. Besides, they might miss me. (*She hurries to her feet*) Don't go! . . . Aaron! (*Her hand stretches out to him.*

She looks back to the house, then to him:) Aaron, stay! . . .
Aaron! (*She looks at her hand: a moment, and then she
throws the colored papers* CAMILLA *gave her, high over her
head into the air. She starts to run over the dune, calling:*)
Wait for me!

The Curtain Falls

ACT TWO

ACT TWO

Scene: The deck of CAMILLA's *beach house. Very early morning.*

Light, air, sky: that is the impression of CAMILLA's *house, which is new and simple and attractively modern. The deck is wide; on one side it descends to a walk from the road; on the other, to the dunes and beach.*

Unlike the neatness at LILY's, *the deck here is littered with* AARON's *boots, plumbing gear, a large old carpetbag, mats for sunning, garden tools, etc. At rear, some old fish nets are hung against the sky. The furniture, however, would be more at home at* LILY's: *in fact, it comes from that house. Old-fashioned, made of wicker, it includes an old swing.*

When the curtain rises, AARON—*wearing a T-shirt and faded suntans—is asleep on the swing. The sun has not been up very long and the light is soft pink, brightening and yellowing during the scene. The front door opens and* NORMA *comes out wearing a soft skirt and blouse and ballet shoes.*

NORMA (*Front*) Good morning! (*She sets the tray of coffee and fruit which she is carrying on a table. She turns to look at* AARON, *and the violin plays very softly. She smiles and kisses him*) Good morning, Prince (*No response. She shakes him*) Aaron! (*He opens his eyes; lets her cheek be kissed by his lips*) I would have let you sleep longer but it's too new. (*Front*) Besides, a marvelous thing happened!

AARON (*Sits up*) Coffee.

NORMA (*Front*) I walked home down the beach, ran right into the dawn and I didn't feel guilty!

AARON Cream.

NORMA (*Front*) I always did before when I came home from a party or something and the sky was opening.

AARON Sugar.

NORMA (*Front*) But today, for the first time in my life, I felt at home in the morning. Even that— (*Indicates the swing*) —didn't make me feel guilty. Oh, Aaron, thank you! (*He nods*) You *are* older than I am. (*Points to her ballet shoes*) And bigger than I am, see? You're lovely. How are you?

AARON Tired. (*He lies down on the deck*)

NORMA (*Front*) Something's wrong.

AARON Until I have my coffee, I don't wake up.

NORMA No. It wasn't good for you.

AARON What?

NORMA (*Indicating the swing*) That.

AARON It was wonderful.

NORMA But it could have been better.

58

AARON It will be.

NORMA It couldn't be. I'm going to have a baby. (*Front*) I am! Every time I read in a book: "That night she conceived," I wondered just how she knew. Well, now *I* know!

AARON How?

NORMA (*Lies down beside him*) Because something that wonderful between two people who love each other has to bear fruit.

AARON You sound as though you were going to have an apple.

NORMA That's a girl's name. I'm going to have a boy.

AARON Think how embarrassed you'd be if you really were going to have a baby.

NORMA (*Front*) He's so experienced! (*To him*) How many times have you been in love?

AARON Never. And I'm not sure I am now.

NORMA I'm sure enough for both of us. You have. (*Front*) Well, beginning Monday morning, he's going to have his coffee *before* I get up.

AARON Why Monday?

NORMA Because Sunday, we're getting married. (AARON *laughs*) We are!
   (*From inside,* CAMILLA *calls out: "Where the hell's the coffee pot?"* NORMA *gets up and starts to go*)

AARON (*Grabs her*)   Out here. (*To* NORMA) Where you running?

NORMA   What's she going to think, me here before breakfast.

AARON   My mother?!
   (*The door opens and out comes* CAMILLA *in her mules, a terry cloth robe and an older, more battered straw hat*)

CAMILLA (*To* NORMA)   Well, you're sure awake now, aren't you, sweetheart?

NORMA   Mrs. Jablonski, I know it's kind of an early hour—

CAMILLA   Oh, you didn't wake me up. A goddam woodpecker did. Which reminds me: I've got to go to the dentist. Where the—

AARON (*Warning*)   Mother.

CAMILLA   heck?—heck's my bathing cap?

AARON   Probably in your book bag.

CAMILLA   Well, where the heck's my goddam book bag?

NORMA (*Finds the bag near the rail*)   Is this it?

60

CAMILLA Ah, thank you.

AARON (*Putting on his boots*) Where're you now?

CAMILLA Sweden.

AARON (*To* NORMA) She reads by countries.

NORMA Why?

CAMILLA Why not? (*Rummaging in the bag*) How's the water, sweetheart?

NORMA I haven't been in yet.

CAMILLA I wouldn't know how else to begin a sunny day. In summer. (*She takes out a bathing cap. Front*) In winter, I walk. Have you ever walked a beach in winter? It's like seeing everything the way it was! (*She takes out a bathing suit*) Anybody down on the beach?

NORMA No.

CAMILLA Good. (*She throws the suit back into the bag*)

AARON (*Front*) Don't worry. She'd wear one if there were.

NORMA (*Front*) I always wear a suit.

CAMILLA Most people do. Except in Sweden.

NORMA We're not in Sweden.

CAMILLA I know. (*Stopping at the top of the beach steps*) Call me Camilla anyway. (*And she goes off*)

NORMA I hope she has a dress to wear.

AARON To our wedding.

NORMA Yes.

AARON (*Front*) You know what happened to the noise of those voices of hers? She's drowned them out—with a medley of fairy tales. (*To* NORMA) The prince wakes the princess with a kiss, and they live happily ever after they have been married in state.

NORMA Right!

AARON (*Gets up*) Wrong. I am no prince. (*Front*) And I told her yesterday I didn't want a wife.

NORMA (*Front*) But he wasn't in love yesterday!

AARON (*Front*) It's too soon to know whether I am today!

NORMA You love me every bit as much as I love you. Now: when two people fall in love, what do they do?

AARON (*Sits*) We've done it.

NORMA They get married.

AARON Why?

NORMA   Why does an apple a day keep the doctor away?

AARON   It doesn't.

NORMA   All right. Why do we go to church on Sundays?

AARON   I don't.

NORMA   (*Front*)   He's an atheist!

AARON   Oh, crap!

NORMA   Aaron!

AARON   What has going to church got to do with believing in
God? What has getting married got to do with being in
love? You know—you don't think, you memorize.

NORMA   You make me feel the way I do when I'm sick in bed
with a fever. The bed tilts up and the floor tilts down. But
I don't have a fever, I have you.

AARON   Ah, Norma . . .

NORMA   Don't you say my name in that tone. (*Front*) When
I was ten, I heard a captain in Fort Riley, Kansas, talk in
that tone. "Ohh, Lady," he said. "Ohh, Lady." He was talking to his horse just before he shot her. (*Suddenly, from
behind the house, there is the boom of a drum*) Oh, Lord!
   (*She starts to run toward the beach steps, but* AARON
stops her)

63

AARON You're always running away. (*Around the corner and up the street ramp comes* CARY. *He stops banging his drum and stares*) I'll be over to fix it in a minute.

CARY Up early, aren't you, Norma dear?

NORMA I've been sleeping so much—

CARY Momma was so surprised. And Schuyler—

NORMA All right: fifty cents.

CARY (*Contemptuously*) Fifty cents?

NORMA How much then? (*He bangs the drum four times*) Two dollars just for not telling Momma and Schuyler??

CARY And the German lady.

AARON What difference if he tells?

CARY There's that wedding on Sunday, boy.

AARON (*To* NORMA) Is there?

NORMA One way or another. My mother has it all arranged and she'd die of humiliation. (*Front*) She's from the South.

AARON (*To* CARY) Go ahead and tell.

CARY But she always pays me not to tell.

64

AARON Well, she isn't going to pay you this time.

CARY Then I'll have to tell.

AARON If you have to, then tell.

CARY But I can't tell!

AARON Why not?

CARY Because if I do, I'm a stool pigeon and nobody's a stool pigeon.

AARON Then don't tell.

CARY But if I don't tell this time, she won't pay me not to tell next time.

NORMA I'll pay you this time.

CARY You will?!

NORMA Yes.

CARY But why should you? Now you know I wouldn't tell anyway. (*Front*) She'd be paying for nothing. She's crazy.

NORMA I am!

CARY (*To* AARON) It's your fault. You changed everything! *You're* crazy! Your mother goes swimming in the ocean without any clothes on!

AARON Doesn't yours?

CARY (*Stops, gasps, giggles, suddenly stops that*) NO!

AARON Don't you?

CARY No!

AARON Not even when nobody's around?

CARY (*Whispers*) It's nasty!

AARON Do you go in the bathtub without your clothes?

CARY Yes.

AARON But not in the ocean?

CARY No!

AARON Then it's the ocean that's nasty.
    (CARY *looks from* AARON *to* NORMA, *then starts running and beating the drum in wild frustration and yelling*)

CARY Youu—arre—CRAZY, CRAZY, CRA—
    (*He pulls up short in front of* CAMILLA *who has just come up from the beach, wet bathing cap in hand*)

CAMILLA Honey, you look all hot and bothered. Why don't you skin out of those clothes and run down for a swim?

66

CARY *(Stares in horror, then banging his drum and yelling, runs off:)* CRAZY, CRAZY, CRAZYYYY.

CAMILLA *(Front)* The sun *is* bright today.
  (She mounts the steps)

NORMA *(Front)* You see? Cary and I are the crazy ones. Crazy to want a bathing suit when we go swimming; crazy to want a wedding when we fall in love. Mrs. Jablonski, don't you think two people who fall in love should have a wedding?

CAMILLA Some people fall in love with people who've already had a wedding.

NORMA *(Front) She's* against weddings too!

CAMILLA No, I'm impartial on that subject.

NORMA Then where's your husband?

AARON What?

NORMA Where's your father?

CAMILLA Why?

NORMA He must be the source!

CAMILLA Of what?

NORMA Of your son's crazy ideas!

CAMILLA Oh, some of his crazy ideas are all his own. (*She picks up the tray*) Why don't we all have breakfast?

NORMA I've had breakfast, thank you.

CAMILLA (*Starting in*) What about lunch?

NORMA At this hour?!?

CAMILLA If you had breakfast and you're hungry, then it's lunch hour. (*She goes in*)

NORMA (*Front*) Maybe these two houses *are* castles; maybe they *are* under a spell; maybe the floors *do* tilt? Or is it the inhabitants who are tilted? But which inhabitants in which house?

CAMILLA (*Coming out again*) How about a nice, cold beer?

NORMA (*To* AARON) Why did you wake me? I wish I could go back to sleep. I wish I were married to Schuyler. And I wish you hadn't come to fix the plumbing.

CAMILLA I wish you'd go swimming. With or without a suit. That's what I do whenever I feel the way you do.

NORMA How can you know how I feel when I don't know how I feel?

CAMILLA That's exactly the feeling I mean. (*Sitting beside her*) And that's when I throw myself into the ocean and float around on my back. The sun warms my top, the water cools my bottom and I say: "All right, Camilla, why are you lost?" Nine times out of ten it's because I've been trying to swim in a school with all the other fish and I need to come up for air. Maybe I'm a little like that first sea thing who said: "Why do we all have to stay in the ocean?" So he waddled and he stumbled and he made it to land. And if he hadn't, we wouldn't be here now . . . Maybe you'd be happier in a school with all the other fish, but why don't you go down there and find out? If you can't float we have a little raft.

AARON   And extra bathing suits.

NORMA   I brought a suit.
    (*A moment, then she goes to the door*)

AARON   Norma!
    (*She stops*)

NORMA   That captain loved his horse, too.
    (*She goes inside*)

CAMILLA   The only thing I can't figure out is the captain's horse.

AARON   He shot her.

CAMILLA   I'm up to date. I take it you've been sounding off against marriage again.

AARON   (*Getting his plumbing gear*)   What's wrong with that?

CAMILLA (*Going and getting a fish net from the rail*) For a boy of twenty it's fine. Particularly for a boy of twenty who happens to be my son.

AARON I don't think I like that remark.

CAMILLA (*Cheerfully*) Then lump it. And tell your friends in the village, I don't mind them hanging their nets here, but they've got to mend them themselves.

AARON Did they ask you to mend them?

CAMILLA (*Sitting on top step, starts to mend the fish net*) No, but you know I can't stand staring at anything with a goddam hole in it. Where are you rushing off to? Your mother-in-law's?

AARON The can is still on the blink.

CAMILLA Take those fool banners and trappings off that horse of yours.

AARON He likes them. They keep the flies away and make him think he's pretty.

CAMILLA They make me think he's hot. You're stuck on Norma.

AARON Who said?

CAMILLA You look at her with a face I never saw before. It's becoming.

AARON (*Sitting beside her*) What do you think of her?

CAMILLA I think she's a nut.

AARON A nice nut.

CAMILLA And a pretty one. And touching.

AARON And gentle.

CAMILLA But a nut. What are you afraid of?

AARON I can wake her with a kiss. I can't change her with a kiss.

CAMILLA What would you change?

AARON Oh—things, ideas.

CAMILLA You haven't told her about your father.

AARON No.

CAMILLA Someone will. (*Front*) People love to be honest about other people.

AARON If I haven't told her, it's only because—

CAMILLA Don't be ashamed! You did nothing except get born.

AARON Mother . . . one or two things I've done, I'm a little ashamed of. But there's nothing you've ever done that I'm the least bit ashamed of.

71

CAMILLA Are you lying?

AARON No, ma'am.

CAMILLA . . . How come you're not ashamed any more?

AARON Like everyone else around here, I got used to it and I love you.

CAMILLA (*After a moment*) My God, I'm glad the old man got stuck with these dunes!
(*Picks up the fish net and starts to go in*)

AARON Hey, Camilla—don't you be ashamed.

CAMILLA Ashamed? Didn't you ever meet my kid?
(*She goes in.* AARON *is picking up his gear when* NORMA, *wearing a bathing suit and high, thick cork-soled beach shoes, comes out of the side door. As they stop and stare at each other, music starts. He puts on his hat with a smile, but she continues to look at him gravely. He is starting slowly toward her when there is the bang of* CARY's *drum. The music stops and* NORMA *hurries down the beach steps.* AARON *hesitates, then is starting after her when* TUCKER *comes up from the street ramp*)

TUCKER Good morning!

AARON Good morning.

TUCKER Whale of a day! (AARON *stares at him*) I'm very responsive to weather.

AARON Arthritis?

TUCKER I meant responsive emotionally. (AARON *just looks at him*) Is Mrs. Camilla Jablonski at home?

AARON If you're looking for a place to rent, I'm afraid we—

TUCKER Oh no. I just want to see Mrs. Jablonski.

AARON O.K. (*He goes to the door*) Hey, Ma. There's a man wants to see you.
 (*He goes around the side of the house.* TUCKER *sees the swing. As he touches it gently, nostalgically, the door opens and* CAMILLA *comes out carrying the coffee pot and mug. One look and she runs back in*)

TUCKER Good morning!
 (*She comes out again*)

CAMILLA You catch me at the damndest times! (*She hands him the mug, puts the coffee pot on a stool, yanks her hat off and dashes for her book bag from which she gets a comb, mirror and lipstick during the next:*) Here: have some coffee. Sit down. Read a book for a minute. Don't look at me. Look at the house.

TUCKER I'll look at the house later. Why don't you sit down and have some coffee?

CAMILLA Go around back and look at my nursery.

TUCKER You're what??

73

CAMILLA My garden. I grow things in sand.

TUCKER How?

CAMILLA By not listening to everybody who said I couldn't.

TUCKER What do you grow?

CAMILLA I started with plants and flowers. I've got quite a little business. Now I'm trying vegetables. If I can grow one little tomato— Tucker, I feel as though you're watching me take a bath.

TUCKER You look wonderful. I can't believe that boy is your son. He looks at least nineteen.

CAMILLA You saw my boy?

TUCKER Just now.

CAMILLA What'd you think of him?

TUCKER Healthy-looking kid.

CAMILLA But what did you think of him?

TUCKER How did you do it?

CAMILLA (*Turns to him*) Do what??

TUCKER You *are* happy.

74

CAMILLA Oh. Sure.

TUCKER But you had such a bad time with your husband.

CAMILLA I did?

TUCKER You wouldn't have gone back to your maiden name otherwise. I'm glad it was bad, Camilla. I'd like to be selfish about you.

CAMILLA Why?

TUCKER I've made so many mistakes. I hardly noticed the day I made one of the biggest.

CAMILLA When *did* you notice, Tucker?

TUCKER Is there someone else now?

CAMILLA I think there are too many people here.

TUCKER Where?

CAMILLA Right here on this deck. There's you and me now, and you and me back there, a century ago.

TUCKER In that swing.

CAMILLA That's a new swing; the old one got rusty long ago. Aren't you getting the four of us mixed up?

TUCKER No, *we* haven't changed.

CAMILLA Tucker, it's morning, there's sunlight, and I see you looking at me and I know what you're seeing. Because I'm looking at you.

TUCKER Don't look *at* me, look *in* me: that's what hasn't changed.

CAMILLA Hasn't it?

TUCKER Why else did you tear off that old hat? Why else did you comb your hair? Why else did you put on lipstick?

CAMILLA . . . You were my first . . . anything.

TUCKER (*A moment, then he gets a chair*) Here: sit down. Now look for me. (*Takes another chair and sits, back to her. She turns*) No—look for me back there. Look for *us* back there. Try, Camilla, please.
  (*The light has begun to pinken to a pool around them. Music*)

CAMILLA I remember without trying.

TUCKER What? Tell me.

CAMILLA Falling asleep on the beach and waking up to see a beautiful young man step into the sunlight.

TUCKER And?

CAMILLA Knowing somehow he wanted me to like him.

TUCKER I did.

CAMILLA And clam digging one day when a lady who knew his wife came by. He got so scared he forgot it was low tide and took a dive right smack on his—

TUCKER Don't remember that.

CAMILLA It was nice.

TUCKER Nice?

CAMILLA He didn't *have* to see me in the daytime. I never did figure out if he did it because he wanted me or because he was such a gentleman. But I'd never had either, so it was nice.

TUCKER Remember more.

CAMILLA The day he went away. To South Dakota.

TUCKER North.

CAMILLA North. I admired you for going.

TUCKER Why?

CAMILLA Because people who inherit money never feel as if they're entitled to it unless they spend their lives making more. But not you. You didn't want the office next to your father's. You were going to raise your kids outdoors, you were going to breed cattle, you were going to— Tucker, did you ever get to North Dakota?

TUCKER Yes.

CAMILLA What happened?

TUCKER I struck oil. (*She laughs*) I did very well in oil. I added three holding companies to the corporation. I did even better in gas. Natural gas.

CAMILLA And came back East.

TUCKER Yes.

CAMILLA He went out there. Who came back?

TUCKER (*Front*) I always remembered her looking up at me without question or criticism.

CAMILLA I loved you.

TUCKER The way women don't look up at a man any more. They can be sitting down, I can be standing above them, but somehow, they manage to look down on me. . . . Why are you looking at me?

CAMILLA I'm not looking at you.

TUCKER You are. At the gray in my hair.

CAMILLA No.

TUCKER You're looking down on me. Turn around.

CAMILLA Maybe it's only the women who have to grow up.

TUCKER Come back!

CAMILLA (*Gets up*) Maybe that's why they look down on you boys. (*Front*) How do you remember somebody? Frozen in space, exactly as they were the last time you saw them. Lying on warm sand or in an old swing, but frozen there. Dead and gone. Tucker, that time is dead and gone.

TUCKER You're wrong. It doesn't have to be.

CAMILLA Five minutes ago when I came out that door holding that pot of coffee, even that time is dead and gone!

TUCKER Two people can bring any time back if they want to, but you don't. Yes, I'm older, I've made mistakes, but what is in me—

CAMILLA Tucker Grogan, one thing I will not let you do! I will not let you slop up the memory of the one man I loved in my whole life. That memory is mine. Who you are now, I don't know. But he belongs to me and you leave him alone!

TUCKER Why are you angry? Because I'm not exactly what you remember?

CAMILLA Because suddenly I'm not sure if you ever were what I remember! And my boy is your—

TUCKER (*After a pause*) I should have figured it out. When you said he was nineteen.

CAMILLA I didn't say he was nineteen. You said he was nineteen.

TUCKER And being nineteen, he has to be my son.

CAMILLA Why?

TUCKER Because we were lovers twenty years ago. He's a fine boy, Camilla!

CAMILLA He's everything my son should be—including twenty. We were lovers twenty-one years ago, Tucker.

TUCKER That's why you're angry. You've never forgiven me!

CAMILLA What for? I had my boy deliberately.

TUCKER . . . Why?

CAMILLA I wanted you for more than just a summer. I wanted some part of you I could love for all the summers. I have that and I thank you.

TUCKER Why didn't you tell me?

CAMILLA I wanted to, but it wouldn't've been fair.

TUCKER Were people very rough on you?

CAMILLA (*Laughs*) No, I was too poor. I think if you're poor enough or rich enough, you can get away with an illegitimate baby. Later on, at school, they made it rough on him.

TUCKER How did he take it?

CAMILLA Oh, he's a fighter. But they were looking at me. A small town has big eyes. People may forgive you what you do for love, but never what you do for pleasure.

TUCKER So there's been no one.

CAMILLA In twenty years? Tucker, I'm a healthy woman.

TUCKER I'm not talking about your health.

CAMILLA Neither am I.

TUCKER Then why haven't you married—I almost said "again"?

CAMILLA That's funny. I think of it as "again," too. Because I never met a man who meant as much as my memory of you. (*Front*) And I wasn't about to get married to prove I'm a success as a woman.

TUCKER I want to do something for our boy. For you.

CAMILLA You've done a lot for me. I learned from you. I made the government pay through the nose for the old man's farm, and these dunes—they're better than your natural gas! Why, I'm practically landed gentry here now! (*Slowly, he takes her in his arms and kisses her. She responds, then puts her head against him. He tilts her chin up but:*) How's your wife?

TUCKER Why do you ask?

CAMILLA (*Smiles*) It was a question that got stuck in my throat that whole summer.

TUCKER You never asked enough of me then. Ask now.

CAMILLA Tucker.

TUCKER Ask.

CAMILLA Are you who I remember?
        (AARON *enters from the side of the house.* CARY *enters from behind* AARON *and sneaks into outdoor shower*)

AARON Whale of a day.

CAMILLA Aaron, this is Mr. Grogan.

TUCKER I'm very glad to meet you, son.

CAMILLA He's an old friend of the family.

AARON How old?

CAMILLA He knew your father.

82

TUCKER (*Shaking* AARON's *hand*) He was a fine man. We were such good friends, a lot of people thought we were very much alike. Didn't they, Camilla?

CAMILLA No one I know.

TUCKER Well, he *was* a fine man. And in his memory, I'd like to do something for you, Aaron. (*Behind them,* NORMA *comes beamishly up the steps from the beach*) A job in my organization.

AARON I've got one right here.

TUCKER I mean a position. There's room for a young man like you.

NORMA (*Front*) *Normally,* a distinguished tycoon does not offer a job to a questionable plumber. *Normally.* (*To* CAMILLA) But nothing is normal any more, is it?

CAMILLA Had a good swim, didn't you?

NORMA (*To* TUCKER) But why *did* you make the offer?

CAMILLA How do you know Mr. Grogan?

NORMA Through his son.

CAMILLA His son?

TUCKER Her fiancé.

CAMILLA *Your* son?

TUCKER My son.

CAMILLA (*Front*) I always hated long explanations.
(*Low drumming starts*)

TUCKER Norma, what are you doing with Aaron?

NORMA (*Finds* CARY *in the shower*) Cary, I'll give you two dollars!

CARY (*Coming out*) You haven't got enough money now. Not all of you put together. (*To* TUCKER) Including you.
(*A bang on the drum and he runs off*)

TUCKER Camilla, my wife came here to see my son married to —(*He turns to see* AARON *fondling* NORMA. CAMILLA *grins*) It won't be funny. She always gets what she wants.

CAMILLA So do I, Tucker.

TUCKER (*Front*) You know, it's sheer luck that any man ever got anywhere. (*To* CAMILLA) What *do* you want?

CAMILLA To see who came back from North *or* South Dakota.

TUCKER North. The man you wanted to.
(*He goes*)

AARON There's a horse's ass for you.

84

CAMILLA Is that so? (*She picks up her straw hat*) Listen. You get one, maybe two chances to take a good bite of life. If you get scared and pass up that chance, you walk around afterwards with a hunger. The kind of hunger that can make anyone a horse's ass. Even you, my darling boy.
(*She puts her hat on* NORMA *and goes in*)

NORMA She's right. You're scared (*Front*) He is. Scared to admit he loves me! Scared to marry me! Scared to leave her and cope with me!

AARON (*Laughs*) Come here!

NORMA *You come here!* You love me, so you get down on one knee and ask me to marry you properly. (AARON *sits in a chair and folds his arms. She sinks to her knees*) *Please!* We'll have such a lovely life, Aaron.

AARON Where?

NORMA Wherever your office is.

AARON What office?

NORMA The office Mr. Grogan is going to give you.

AARON (*Rising and going to her*) Norma, I told that man—

NORMA I cannot marry a plumber!

AARON I'm not a plumber! I'm in real estate! (*Front*) I am!! We rent the old farmhouse to her mother. I built this house

85

last fall. This fall, I'll build another. That means two houses to rent next summer and we own enough dune land to build six more.

NORMA   And when the last one is built?

AARON   I retire.

NORMA   At thirty??

AARON   At twenty-five!

NORMA   You have no ambition!

AARON   Do you?

NORMA   I'm a girl. I don't have to have any. You must want something.

AARON (*Kneeling beside her*)   I do. I want to look around the world and see what other people are up to. Think what fun we could have! Going anyplace and everyplace *before* we have children!

NORMA   You have to be married to have children. (*He laughs and kisses her*) Oh, ask me to marry you. I don't want to be peculiar. I want a wedding, with bridesmaids in lovely yellow dresses.

AARON   On Sunday.

NORMA (*Front*)   For the first year, I want a two-and-a-half room apartment with a sunken living room and a *budget!*

86

AARON Near my office.

NORMA (*Front*) And the next year, he'll get a good raise and I'll get a good maid and we'll move to Connecticut. We'll convert a barn for the children.

AARON (*Front*) Three.
(*Softly, a violin begins the bugle call "Lights Out"*)

NORMA One of the boys will go to West Point—Daddy's name will help—and the other will go into business. (*She yawns*) Aaron'll be a vice-president, by then. Maybe even in politics. Why not? (*Another yawn*) Excuse me. A senator. Do you have to be born in Connecticut to be a senator from Connecticut? (*Trailing off*) Do you? Do you have to be born . . .
(*Her head goes back against* AARON, *her voice fades away with the last notes of the violin. She is asleep. Awkwardly, he inches back on his knees to lower her head carefully to the floor. There, he has to give it a twist so she can rest on her cheek.* CAMILLA *comes out and takes a good look at* NORMA)

CAMILLA You must be one helluva lover.

AARON (*Placing a pillow under* NORMA) Did you know you're the mother of a future senator from Connecticut?

CAMILLA Tomorrow the world.
(*She begins to fertilize some plants*)

87

AARON I've never been afraid in my life. I am now. I can't have her and all this and I'm afraid of losing one or the other.

CAMILLA Are you sure you want this?

AARON How is it you don't ask me if I'm sure I want her?

CAMILLA Oh—I just wonder if because you know how much I like all this, you feel you have to like it, too.

AARON Listen, I love all this! I have it all year round while everyone else has to work their behinds off to get it for two picayune weeks a summer. If I came here from the city, built two houses—at my age—everybody'd be saying to Norma: that boy's a real smart operator. Why don't they say it about me?

CAMILLA Because you're doing it for the wrong reason: you like it.

AARON Why should I be doing it?

CAMILLA To get rich.

AARON I don't want to be rich, I want to be surprised. I don't want everything to be laid out, including me. I don't want a two-and-a-half split-level sunken living room—
     (NORMA *begins to stir*)

CAMILLA Two boys and a girl—

88

AARON All named Junior—

CAMILLA You convert the barn—

AARON Become a senator from Connecticut—

CAMILLA And die of sleeping sickness. I see it all.
(*Behind them,* NORMA *has awakened*)

AARON It's what she wants.

CAMILLA It's what she *knows*. Marvelous as you are, even you can't change her overnight. (*Front*) He can't. It's as though her mother and her brothers and her cousins and her aunts, as though everyone she knows is in the Army just as her father was. And Aaron and I? Conscientious objectors. There they all are, the whole kit and kaboodle of the world, marching along, calling out to her: "Norma, come march with us!" And here he is, going his own sweet cockeyed way, singing: "Come dance with me." (*To* AARON) Dancing's hard. And all those marchers, they want you to be in uniform, too. If you don't march when they holler, they make it tough on you.

AARON I know.

CAMILLA Not yet, you don't.

AARON I won't march.

CAMILLA It's much easier.

AARON I don't care.

CAMILLA It's safer.

AARON I don't want to be safe.
    (*She kisses him*)

CAMILLA But if you want her, you might have to change some
of your—
    (*She sees* NORMA *listening*)

NORMA (*To* AARON) Come march with me.
    (*A moment, then he goes to her. Quietly:*)

AARON I can't.

NORMA Please, Aaron.

AARON No.

NORMA (*Front*) Do you realize that in less than one day, I've
been jilted twice?

AARON And in less than one day, you've fallen asleep twice?

NORMA Was I asleep again? (*Front*) Who did it?

AARON A senator from Connecticut.

CAMILLA Sweetheart, you did it yourself. (NORMA *gets up*)
You always do. That first thing from the sea—

NORMA (*Front*) She's going to tell me to go swimming again!

CAMILLA You can swim, dance, walk, fly, whatever you want! (*Front*) That's what almost everybody says and almost nobody does because it's so damned hard. (*To* NORMA) But *you* can do it. *You* can dance!

NORMA Mrs. Jablonski, I like you very much, but I'm Norma Brown. I can't call you Camilla, I can't dance—(*To* AARON) And I can't go traveling with a man who doesn't want to get married. (*Front*) It's all very lovely for them to say: Do whatever you want. Well, you know what I want? I want to get dressed and go home to my mother!
 (*And tearfully she storms into the house*)

CAMILLA And Prince Charming stands like a lump.

AARON Can you see what she'd do if I told her you were never married?

CAMILLA She might stay awake.

AARON Why are you pushing me?

CAMILLA I think you are ashamed. I think you're afraid that if you tell her about me, you'll lose her.

AARON Yes, I'm afraid of that. But more of something else.

CAMILLA What?

AARON   That if I lose her because of that, it would hurt you.
(*Drumming—and* CARY *enters and* NORMA *appears*)

CARY   I have a communiqué for Mrs. C. Jablonski.

CAMILLA   Who from?

CARY   The enemy.

CAMILLA   I'll see that she gets it. (*She reads the note*) "Dear
Mrs. Jablonski, forgive me for not being a good neighbor
sooner. Would you and your son do me the honor—"

CARY   Mrs. Grogan put that in.

CAMILLA   "—the honor of dining with us this evening at eight.
Cordially, Lily Brown."

CARY   You didn't read down in the corner.

CAMILLA   Excuse me. "Black tie." *Full* uniform.

CARY   She wants a R.S.V.P. for the cook before the market
closes.

CAMILLA   (*Looks to* AARON)   Well?

AARON   Tell her no.

CAMILLA   One horse's ass in the family is enough. Tell her yes!
(CARY *starts to drum*)

NORMA You don't know those women.

CAMILLA And they don't know me! (*To* CARY *as she puts one of her hats on his head*) Tell her we'll be there at eight. (*He drums louder as she crosses toward the house*) I better see what there is for supper. I always like to eat *before* the show!

    (*The drum is thundering*)

The Curtain Falls

ACT THREE

ACT THREE

Scene: The deck at LILY'S.

Early evening. The last sunlight is glowing on the three people who are asleep on the deck. All are dressed in dinner clothes; DEEDEE, *in the inevitable glittering pajamas, sits asleep in a chair next to* LILY. TUCKER *is asleep by a backgammon table.*

As the curtain rises, CARY, *with* CAMILLA's *hat on his head, stares at each of the sleepers in turn. He claps his hand over his mouth to suppress his giggles and, stopping in front of* DEEDEE, *stares at her. Suddenly, he drops his pants, sticks his thumbs in his ears and belly-rolls at her. Instantly, a cracking roll of thunder. The sleepers do not move, but* CARY *gasps, hurriedly picks up his pants and looks up to the sky as though he had been caught by God. Then, he comes down front and begins to talk—like* CAMILLA.

CARY   Many thanks. Sweetheart, when I got troubles and I want to figure 'em out, I just throw myself in that ocean down there. That's how I get rid of 'em: in that big old ocean, floating bare-ass.

LILY   Inside and wash your mouth out with soap!
   (CARY *runs in, leaving the hat on the porch*)

DEEDEE   (*To* LILY)   You've ruined the rehearsal.

LILY   My child is not going to pick up such language!

97

DEEDEE I rather like "bare-ass."

LILY You may have brought up your children—

DEEDEE Are you implying my children are ill-bred?

LILY Schuyler is a perfect gentleman.

DEEDEE Oh, but I'm not a lady!
　　　(*They move to each other like panthers*)

LILY I was not saying—

DEEDEE What are you saying?

LILY Merely that I do not think—

DEEDEE Indeed you don't!

LILY If the General were alive—

DEEDEE He wouldn't dare hit me.

LILY I could just open my mouth and scream!

DEEDEE Take a tranquilizer. These days, it's not only unneces-
sary to be nervous, it's stubborn. Now: let's rehearse our
sleeping again.

SCHUYLER (*Enters: to* TUCKER) Found the dice.

98

Jeffrey Rowland, Madeleine Sherwood, Richard Derr
and Eileen Heckart, as CARY, LILY, TUCKER, and DEEDEE

DEEDEE Schuyler, put down those dice. You put Norma to sleep. Darling, I know it's embarrassing but it's even more embarrassing that a little sea urchin woke her up. (*Front*) That's why Norma is grateful to him. But once the boy and his mother come here and put us to sleep, Norma will see how dreary and common they are. (*A crack of thunder*) Schuyler, I am not doing all this for myself, I'm doing it for you.

SCHUYLER That's the first time I've ever heard you speak like a mother.

DEEDEE This is an emergency. Here's your fiancée, tossing you aside like an old salad—

LILY And for who?

DEEDEE A plumber boy.
(*They move to each other like purring kittens*)

LILY No social position at all.

DEEDEE Well, with that mother!

LILY And that father!

DEEDEE Who is the father anyway?

LILY I don't know, but with that mother—

DEEDEE How right you are! (*Kisses* LILY) Now: places every-one!

SCHUYLER (*Gets up*)   All this is crazy! And unethical. It was unethical to unvite the Jablonskis to a black-tie dinner in the first place.

DEEDEE   Should we exchange our manner of living for theirs?

SCHUYLER   No. But you know how foolish they'll look—

LILY (*Front*)   What is really worrying him is: How could Norma be in love with him one day and the very next with that piece of riffraff. Well, the answer is simple. No daughter of mine could *ever* be in love with a plumber!

TUCKER (*Going to the bar*)   He is not a plumber and he is not riffraff! He's a nice boy and he's in real estate.

DEEDEE   He's a plumber.

TUCKER   He builds houses.

DEEDEE   He plumbs.

TUCKER   Deedee, I've met him. He's a nice boy.

DEEDEE (*Rises*)   Tucker, meet this boy. This is Schuyler Grogan, your son. I did not fly several thousand miles to not go to his wedding. (*To* SCHUYLER) You expend so much energy being correct and conventional, you don't have a drop left to make love to that girl!

SCHUYLER   This is between Norma and me. I have to find out exactly what I am to her.

DEEDEE Oh, I can tell you right now what you are to her. You're a sleeping pill, that's what you are!

SCHUYLER One thing you and I do have in common: we've always been disappointed in each other.

DEEDEE (*Front*) These days, it's too common for a mother and son to have that in common. I have never been defeated in my life, Schuyler. I will not let you be defeated in yours. Let's have that in common.

LILY Bravo!

SCHUYLER And Mrs. Jablonski won't let Aaron be defeated in his, I suppose. What about Norma?

LILY (*Rises*) I'll take care of Norma.

SCHUYLER (*Front*) That's what I like about mothers: They think children are children.
        (*Goes off*)

DEEDEE (*To* LILY) Why do we have them?

LILY Why, because we're supposed to, honey! We have to do *something!*
        (TUCKER *laughs and goes in*)

DEEDEE Don't you ever say that in front of a man again.
        (*From offstage comes a woman's voice chanting the bugle call for assembly*)

LILY   What's that?

DEEDEE   *Danke schön,* Elisabet! (*To* LILY) Your daughter's coming. Soften her up. (*The bugling continues*) *Danke!* (*The bugling stops*) Remember: pretend that what Norma wants, you want. Her happiness is your happiness.

LILY   (*By rote*)   "Her happiness is my happiness."

DEEDEE   Put the other side on the defensive and they do just what you want them to. I know. And I'm the only woman I know who has never been divorced.

LILY   I was never divorced.

DEEDEE   Yes, but your husband died on you, Flora dear.
         (*She exits through one door as* NORMA *comes out through the other in low heels and a simple frock*)

LILY   (*Angrily*)   "Your happiness is my happiness! Your happiness is my happiness!" And you're not dressed. I have planned an elaborate party, it is fifteen till eight and you are not dressed!

NORMA   I think I look nice.

LILY   Not nice enough for my plans—oh, I could murder that woman! She has called me every flower in the garden but the one I was named for! It's her way of showing her lack of respect for me!

NORMA   Be happy: she'll be gone soon.

LILY Sometimes I think no one has had any respect for me since your daddy died. As though that was my fault! You know I am giving a formal dinner and there you are, in that tacky dress and slippers! Why you are not wearing shoes with heels is— (*Stops, remembering her orders. Suddenly sweet*) Oh, darling. Is Joshua very much shorter than you are?

NORMA His name is Aaron.
  (*She has picked up* CAMILLA's *hat and looks at it curiously*)

LILY There was a woman down home who married a dwarf. But he was of good family. (*Takes the hat away from* NORMA *as:*) Your grandmomma, my momma—rest her loving soul—she used to say that it behooved a lady to choose a man she can look up to. Well, I suppose you can manage to keep sitting.

NORMA I can look up to Aaron without sitting.

LILY Then why aren't you wearing heels? And why that dress?

NORMA I want his mother to feel comfortable.

LILY So you are dressing for her, not me. Well, do as you will. Your happiness is my happiness.

NORMA (*Front*) Why do I tremble every time she says that? (*During the next, they follow each other about, unconsciously emptying the same ash trays, rearranging the same chairs*)

LILY Oh, we are all nervous—what with the wedding so imminent and all the preparations and arrangements that have to be changed for your Mr. Jablonski—I wish he'd be cooperative enough to change his name. You'd think his father would have by now, it's so un-American somehow. Why isn't he coming?

NORMA Who?

LILY The father.

NORMA Where?

LILY To dinner.

NORMA You didn't ask him.

LILY But I was told he wasn't there.

NORMA He isn't.

LILY Then how could I ask him?

NORMA You couldn't.

LILY Well, that's why I didn't. (*Front*) Now why do I feel I just bought something I don't need. Norma—

NORMA I'll change my dress.

LILY Norma, why isn't he there?

NORMA   Who?

LILY   The father, that's who. Why doesn't he live with them?

NORMA   I don't know.

LILY   Where does he live?

NORMA   I don't know.

LILY   Is he dead?

NORMA   I don't know.

LILY   What does he do? Where is he from? Who is he? You don't know. Do you know anything about him?

NORMA   No.

LILY   Well, don't you care? Haven't you asked?

NORMA   I've told you. Aaron does not want to get married.

LILY   Twaddle!

NORMA   He doesn't. But even if he changes his mind and I accept, I will be marrying him, not his father.

LILY   Hogwash! You think all my talk about family is Lily Brown being a middle-class snob. Well, there are such words as hereditary and congenital, my dear—I wouldn't be surprised to find out he's been put away. The father, I mean.

(*Front*) Well, I wouldn't! From all I hear, that woman could have driven him to it. And it is certainly one explanation of a son who gallops up and down the beach on an overdressed horse—what are you doing?

NORMA You forgot to take down the flag.

LILY (*After a moment; low*) Oh, Bert! . . . This is the first and only time I have forgotten since your daddy passed over. That's the state you have gotten me into, missy.

NORMA I'm sorry. I—

LILY Hush!
(*And she starts to bugle until the flag is down*)

NORMA (*Folding the flag and going toward the house*) I'll put on high heels.

LILY Just don't call me Rose.

NORMA Mother, why do you want so much for me to marry Schuyler?

LILY (*Closing the backgammon set*) Have you looked at this backgammon set of the Grogans? Real ivory, real jade!

NORMA Yes, they're rich.

LILY Monogrammed!

NORMA Very rich. What good is all that—

106

LILY Go no further with that sentence! Your happiness is my happiness—but when you start questioning what good is money! My darling, money is just lovely! (*Kisses her, then: front*) And anyone who says it isn't, is suffering with indigestion from sour grapes. Maybe you can't buy happiness, but you can certainly sell it!

NORMA But suppose I love Aaron and don't love Schuyler—

LILY (*Folding the flag in military fashion*) Love! You know who ends up in the divorce courts? People who married for love, that's who. Marriage is an institution and no institution was ever built on love. No, ma'am! (*She puts the flag in the house but comes right out again. Front:*) You know what love is? Sex. Sex pure and simple. That's all it is, that's all it ever was, that's all it ever will be. Two human beings quivering and panting like animals at the water hole. They slake their thirst and divorce. I have seen it at all ages. I see it now, shaking all over her like fringe.

NORMA That is not what it is!

LILY Don't contradict me, I'm your mother. But because I am your mother, do not think sex is a mystery to me. I am not a frigid woman. I have known the time and the place for sex. It's only a mystery to all those people who spend too much time at it in too many places! They are forever falling in love until the culmination! Then they are on the prowl again. And why? Because love is sex and sex is just a matter of losing your mind for a few minutes— where are you going?

NORMA Upstairs to change.

LILY You sit right down and listen to me.

NORMA No! In two minutes, you'll be telling me what your marriage to Daddy was *really* like!

LILY My marriage to your daddy was perfect! He gave me a position and I improved his.

NORMA But didn't you ever—

LILY Quiver and pant, no, I did not!

NORMA But in the beginning, when he first came along, *that* was exciting, wasn't it?

LILY It was not; it was a relief. What counter have you been getting your notions at? You want me to have been swept off my young feet! You want me to say now that life is what? An exciting adventure! Honey, only children think that. Life is the same as always, and no inventions invented ever change it. (*Front*) You laugh some, you cry some; you're sick, you're well; you get some of this, you don't get some of that; you die. That's life.

NORMA May I go up and change now?

LILY No you may not! (*Sitting. Quietly:*) What is the matter with you?! I'm not really asking, because I know. What did you do last night? Don't tell me. Well, apparently you have not satisfied your desire.

NORMA (*Hushed*) I don't know you.

LILY What else is that boy with that awful name good for? You have not satisfied it, you cannot transfer it and you cannot control it. Well, if you concentrated in your head for once, you would see that you can have both.

NORMA Both what?

LILY Let me point out to you that you have this night and tomorrow night.

NORMA For what?

LILY To use.

NORMA Use?

LILY For whatever will enable you to marry Schuyler on Sunday.

NORMA What are you telling me? You're my mother!

LILY It is because I am your mother that I am telling you not to be a quivering idiot.

NORMA For which reason? Is it that you really believe I would be so terribly wrong to marry Aaron?

LILY Yes!

NORMA Or is it . . . is it that you don't want me to have what you never had?

LILY   And what is that?

NORMA   Love.

LILY   Nonsense! (*Starting for the house*) And in less than an hour from now, you will see what nonsense that— (*She suddenly cracks* NORMA *hard across the face on her way in, then stops at the door*) Do you know what love is? Or is it that you have just learned what sex is?
(*Goes in.* NORMA *remains perfectly still, a few tears trickling down her cheeks.* CARY *comes out from around the side of the house*)

CARY   I told you you were going to get it! (*A crack of thunder. Yelling up:*) O.K.! I didn't mean I was *glad* she got it. (*To* NORMA) I just said you would get it and you did. I don't like that Aaron. (SCHUYLER *appears on the path from the beach. He stands, looking at* NORMA *who sits quietly. After a moment, she turns and looks at* SCHUYLER. *They hold the look as* CARY *moves a step between them, folds arms, then:*) You look better with Schuyler, Norma. You look right with him. (*Goes to* SCHUYLER. *Low:*) For Pete's sake, don't put her to sleep!
(*And he jumps off the deck and runs off*)

SCHUYLER   I think I should warn you—they're planning more than a dinner.

NORMA   What?

SCHUYLER   It wouldn't be ethical for me to betray them.

NORMA (*Annoyed*) I don't care what they're planning! There's nothing they can do!
(*She gets up and starts in*)

SCHUYLER (*Angrily runs up to block her way*) Crap! . . . That's the approach, isn't it? Norma, there are four seasons, and only one is summer. Where do you think you're going with that boy? Fishing?

NORMA He's in real estate.

SCHUYLER He's built one house!

NORMA He wants to travel.

SCHUYLER That means passports and injections and stomach trouble!

NORMA You're angry! Is that why you want to kiss me?

SCHUYLER I always do.

NORMA But now more than ever. And you want to marry me more than ever. Why?

SCHUYLER Males are naturally competitive. I want to win.

NORMA I'm glad that's all it is, because you lose.
(*She starts past him. He grabs her violently and kisses her, but she breaks away*)

SCHUYLER You're not in love with him. It's sex, that's all it is.

NORMA (*Front*) He's in on it with my mother!
(*He grabs her and kisses her again. A moment, and this time she returns the kiss. Softly:*)

NORMA What happened to your principles?

SCHUYLER I love you despite them.

NORMA (*Front*) My, this is confusing! (*She looks at* SCHUYLER. *There is the same music as when she first met* AARON) Very confusing!
(*He laughs as she hurries into the house, and* DEEDEE *appears*)

SCHUYLER I'm going to marry her!
(*He starts off*)

DEEDEE Schuyler . . . (*He turns. Lightly:*) I rather love you.

SCHUYLER I rather love you, Mother.
(*He goes as* TUCKER *comes out*)

DEEDEE It's drink time! (*She sits as* TUCKER *prepares drinks*) We're going to win, Tucker! Your son has finally bestirred himself—and that boy is an absolute Niagara of emotion underneath all that control! I'm his mother and I know. (*Front*) I remember telling his psychiatrist that. Not that she listened. That woman was so hostile! To this day, I regret letting Schuyler continue with her, particularly— thank you. (*For her champagne*) Particularly after he caught that big Viennese cow asleep in her chair during his hour.

(*Front*) Well, Norma is what he needs. Norma is what he wants, Norma is what he's going to have. (*To* TUCKER) No, I haven't met his rival and I haven't seen the mother for years—and then only through binoculars. But Elisabet has told me enough. I can imagine what the father is like. Or was like. A snappy dapper little traveling salesman for the hulking farmer's daughter.

TUCKER She was not hulking.

DEEDEE She certainly was hulking. I can still hear that hulk clomp clomp clomping into the kitchen. It was directly beneath my bedroom. I lay there swollen and ugly and I could hear that huge hulk clomping every time she delivered those bushels of potatoes. My God, the amount of potatoes that enormous hulk delivered! We could have sold them for surplus! Well, that type would never have married a dandy. No, she would have cast her big net and pulled in some weak little idealist who thought he was embracing Mother Earth. (TUCKER *makes himself a second drink*) In less than a year, he would have been driven to drink. Tucker, a conversation is not a monologue, you know. I don't doubt you made more of a contribution in the days when you were frolicking over the dunes in gay pursuit of your Potato Queen. (*Front*) I've never been able to understand rapture on the sand. Isn't it awfully gritty? (*To* TUCKER) But you were so aglow with ideals yourself in those beachy days, I'm sure the lady was impressed. Not too impressed, though, come to think of it. I mean after all, how soon after you did she marry and have that misbegotten son?

TUCKER He's nineteen.

DEEDEE He's twenty. Norma told me he was two years younger than she, and she's twenty-two. (*Front*) Of course, when most people tell you their age, I immediately add five. That would make him twenty-five. But then she would have been carrying him in a rack on her back the summer we were here. And that would have gotten in the way of her thrashing around the dunes with you, wouldn't it, dear? No, the boy is twenty. And we were here in the summer of—why, Tucker, the fair lady couldn't have been very much impressed with you at all! Because we were here in the summer of . . . (*A very long pause*) How you must have laughed at me.

TUCKER No.

DEEDEE All these years, how you have been laughing at me.

TUCKER I didn't know myself until this morning.

DEEDEE You didn't have to know to laugh. But she knew; she has been laughing. That's why you offered the boy a job. I will see him in hell first. Schuyler is your son, Tucker. Your only son. He wants Norma. He has got to get what he wants. (*Pause*) I think you will now get me another drink.

TUCKER (*Takes her glass, kisses her hand. Then:*) Deedee . . . it happened a long long time ago.

DEEDEE Oh, not to me, Tucker. To me, it happened just a moment ago. And it will take me a long long time to forget it.

(From inside the house comes a long, low rapid drum roll—the kind associated with a march to the guillotine. Out one door comes LILY; *up the beach ramp comes* SCHUYLER; *last is* NORMA, *dressed in a lovely dinner gown and high heels. Everyone faces the side leading to the entrance from the road. The drum stops and* CAMILLA *and* AARON *enter. Somehow, they make the others look overdressed.* AARON *wears a casual comfortable summer suit with a black bow tie.* CAMILLA's *dress might have been a dressing gown fixed over for the occasion, but she looks cool and soft and very lovely. There is a long silence during which* CAMILLA *has the ease and patience of someone waiting for a graduation exercise to begin. Finally, she looks at* NORMA—*and winks)*

NORMA Mother . . .

LILY Oh; welcome! Do make yourselves at home. But this is your home! Well, house. You know everybody, of course.

DEEDEE They don't know me.

LILY A thousand pardons! This is Mrs. Grogan.

DEEDEE I have been looking forward to this meeting . . . *Miss* Jablonski.

CAMILLA I've been looking forward to it myself, Mrs. Grogan.
     (She sits)

LILY *(Suddenly to* DEEDEE) Did you say "Miss Jablonski"?

TUCKER Why don't we have dinner?

CAMILLA (*To* TUCKER) Sea air makes everyone hungry.

DEEDEE For one thing or another, Miss Jablonski.

LILY (*Front*) A note of confusion is ringing in my ears. Twice I have heard this lady referred to as "Miss" Jablonski, but not once have I heard either correction or objection.

CAMILLA Two things I object to: titles and labels.

DEEDEE But you entitle yourself "Mrs." Jablonski.

CAMILLA Oh, no. I have a son, so other people give me that label, automatically. I'm Camilla Jablonski.

LILY Yes, but are you—

AARON If you need a title, the right one is "Miss."

NORMA (*Front*) The floor is tilting again.

LILY "Miss"?

DEEDEE It simply means—

CAMILLA It simply means I was never married. My boy is illegitimate.

LILY You mean—

CAMILLA I mean if she marries him, she won't have a father-in-law.

NORMA (*Who has been staring at* CAMILLA) Why?

AARON (*To* CAMILLA) You don't have to explain.

CAMILLA Have a drink.

TUCKER Would you like one?

CAMILLA I'm fine and dandy. (*Front*) What the hell! It's no shock to me.

NORMA (*To* CAMILLA) The man was killed before you could marry. In a terrible plane crash or a war or—

AARON He was married already.

NORMA (*To* CAMILLA) But you didn't know.

AARON She knew.

NORMA His wife wouldn't divorce him.

AARON You want excuses and she doesn't need any.

NORMA But I do!

AARON Yes! (*To* CAMILLA) You see?!

NORMA *I* see! You *wanted* me to be shocked. Well, I am! Go on: be delighted!

CAMILLA He isn't.

NORMA He is! Now he has a really good excuse for running away from marriage!

LILY Like mother, like son.

NORMA He's not like her; she's strong! (*Kneeling by* CAMILLA) You won't even make up an excuse. But you were desperately in love with him, weren't you?

CAMILLA (*Smiles*) Yes, I was in love with him.

NORMA (*Front*) Well, *that's* something! What was he?

DEEDEE What he was is of no importance.

LILY You mean he was of no importance.

DEEDEE What I mean is what he was doesn't matter.

LILY I beg to dif—

DEEDEE Don't. The father could be president of the Stock Exchange, the son is still illegitimate.

LILY Illegitimate or not, the son of a president is a horse of a different color from the son of a plumber. I'm certain that boy's father was a nobody! (*To* CAMILLA) If that angers you, then simply tell us: who was he?

TUCKER I think dinner—

DEEDEE *(Rises)* So do I!

LILY No, I want to know! Who was he? And where is he now, whoever he is?

CAMILLA . . . I'm afraid he's dead.

DEEDEE Dead?

TUCKER Dead?

CAMILLA Dead.

TUCKER Just what did he die of?

CAMILLA Natural causes.

TUCKER Such as.

CAMILLA Not living like he wanted to.

DEEDEE Indeed!

LILY I thought you said natural causes.

CAMILLA That's a very natural cause. You'd be surprised how many people stop living from just that.

TUCKER I don't believe that man is dead at all.

LILY Neither do I. She is simply trying to conceal the fact that her son's other parent was of equally low origin.

AARON My mother's were lower, but she's something neither of you are.

DEEDEE And what is that?

AARON A lady.

LILY Well! An insolent mother breeds an insolent son!

DEEDEE (*To* TUCKER, *who moves forward*) Be still.

LILY I will not be still!

TUCKER Excuse me, Lily.

LILY No, sir. That is my daughter who is fluctuating on the brink of disaster, not yours! (*To* NORMA *as* TUCKER *goes in*) You think once you pass twenty-one, you can discharge me. I am your mother, not a housekeeper! If you are tired of my services, then pay the bill that is due, and that bill must be paid in respect to me, not to that disgusting woman! (*To* CAMILLA) Yes, ma'am, disgusting is what you are! It is polite for what you are. (*Front*) Why she didn't even have the decency to invent a husband and a married name! You think it was because she is so honest? No, there is a face to society that must be preserved but that woman prefers to spit in it! (*To* CAMILLA) How dare you go swimming in a public ocean without clothing? And don't tell me it is simply honesty to term your condition in that public water as "bare-ass"! (*Front*) An ass is also called a "behind"—and easier. And there are words such as "naked" and "nude"—

NORMA Mother, please!

LILY Daughter, please! Are you going to tell me to be still now? You are lacking in respect, missy, and it's your respect that I demand!

DEEDEE Demand first what you can get. Is it her respect? Or is it her marriage to Schuyler? You ramble like a rose, Lily. And you don't get results. (*To* NORMA) Now: you read when you're under the dryer in the beauty parlor, don't you?

NORMA Yes.

DEEDEE Movie magazines, women's magazines.

NORMA Yes.

DEEDEE Don't. (*Front*) That's like having your brain washed and waved along with your hair. That's why she insists on regarding Miss Jablonski as a heroine who has borne the fruit of a great love. What the girl needs is a plain statement of the plain truth. (*To* CAMILLA) And the plain truth is that a bitch mother breeds a bastard son.

NORMA No!

AARON (*Simultaneously*) That's enough.

DEEDEE The result of self-indulgence—

AARON *Mother!*

DEEDEE —carelessness and self-indul—

CAMILLA *Sit down and shut up! Both of you!* (DEEDEE *and* LILY *sit.* CAMILLA, *rises, paces, breathing hard, getting control*) Not a word, not a word till I bring myself up from your level. (*Front*) There's a story they make me think of. About a woman, a woman taking a sunbath in a meadow, nude. (*To* LILY) That word all right? (*Front*) This woman was lying there, happy, minding her own business when she felt something on her breast. (*To* LILY) That word all right? (*Front*) She looked down and there was an ant walking over it. Well, a little ant never hurt anyone, so she lay back and enjoyed the sun some more. Pretty soon, the ant brought over a friend, a beetle, and the two of them were walking over her breast. The beetle was kind of big, but no real bother, so she paid no mind. Just closed her eyes, and was dozing off when along came a wasp and stung her right on the tip. *"That does it,"* she said. "EVERYBODY OFF!" (*To* NORMA) Including you, sweetheart. You want an excuse for my life. If I didn't make one up twenty years ago for my son, don't think I'm about to now. What I did, I did because it was right for me. There's a little bell inside that tells you what's right for you. When it rings, you open your door and *go!* (DEEDEE *yawns elaborately.* LILY *follows her leader and they both "go to sleep."*) These two never listened to it, these two sleeping beauties. And they're too angry to hear it now because, you know, outside of her blue hair and her Southern mouth, there isn't a helluva lot of difference between them. They both set out in the same boat to the standard ports of call. Oh, she traveled in a suite— (LILY *opens her eyes*) —and you only had a cabin. (*A glare from* DEEDEE *sends* LILY *"back to sleep." Then, front:*) But they both had the same .thought: "Is that all there is to the journey? Isn't there something missing? No:

everybody else is on board, everybody else is traveling the same line to the same port. This is all there is." And just then, just then *I* come along. I fly my own flag, I sail my own ship to any port I choose, and what do you know? I'm riding free on the wind, *I'm enjoying it and*—THAT— JUST—KILLS THEM!!

(DEEDEE's *eyes flash open. Quickly, she stretches and smiles*)

DEEDEE   Kills who? Have I missed something?

NORMA   I hope not. I wouldn't have missed it for the world!

DEEDEE *(Front)*   She insists on regarding that rejected woman as the heroine.

NORMA *(Front)*   Oh, no, I'm the heroine. This is about me.

DEEDEE *(Rises)*   This is more important than just you.

CAMILLA   What could be more important?
(TUCKER *comes out*)

DEEDEE   What you refuse to believe in and try to ignore: the family! You can refuse to believe in God, too, but you can't ignore Him either. And here—the family is God!

CAMILLA *(Touching* AARON*)*   We're a family.

DEEDEE   Not legally, darling, not socially.

NORMA   They're mother and son, and they're happy. Doesn't that matter?

DEEDEE No.

CAMILLA No??

DEEDEE *No.*

CAMILLA (*Descending steps. Front*) Listen—anybody with her values, look out! Maybe they meant something once upon a time, but that was before taxes.

DEEDEE (*Coming down to her. Front*) Ask this heroine whether she was living so free and gallant or just being damn selfish! Why, she was so busy making her nose and thumb inseparable that she left a mark on her child for him to pass on to his children! And not a strawberry mark either!

CAMILLA There is no mark on him!

DEEDEE He isn't the lost heir to a king, he won't live palatially ever after!

CAMILLA Careful: he could!

DEEDEE He could not!

CAMILLA Not legally?

DEEDEE Not socially! That takes more than a crown of gold! We have no kings, but you behave as though we have no family and no blood!

CAMILLA We *all* have blood and we *do* have kings! Anyone can be king in his own kingdom with a crown of his own pride! My son is prince in my house—and tomorrow he will be king in his own!

DEEDEE Built on sand like yours! You want to give him a crown, you didn't even give him a name!

CAMILLA He has *my* name, and my father's and my grand-father's—

DEEDEE A name that means nothing and has no tradition! (*Going to* SCHUYLER) Well, my son has his father's name and through me alone, he comes from a tradition, from a family, from a long line of fisher folk as clean as the seas they sailed!

TUCKER Your family ran a fish store in Pawtucket, Rhode Island.
     (*A moment*)

LILY (*Front*) No one is what they seem any more. Just no one!

DEEDEE (*Quietly, to* SCHUYLER) Your father barks because he identifies with the underdog. Well, I wasn't born with blue hair either. Very few of us are born as luckily as you, Tucker. Even fewer do anything about it. That takes hard work and drive and imagination. In Pawtucket, Rhode Island, I was dead. (*To* CAMILLA) I brought myself to life, to a life you wish you had! (*To* NORMA) To a life you can have! (*Front*) Yes, my pearls *are* real! My hair *is* blue!

125

I now *do* come from a long line of fisher folk! And by the time that girl has my grandchildren, I shall come from a line that goes back to Amerigo Vespucci and Vasco Di-Gamma! (*To* TUCKER) It took damned hard work to convert myself into what was finally pleasing to your family. If it didn't please you, why didn't you stop me?

TUCKER I've always tried to please too many people.

DEEDEE You stood up when you married me despite them. Why have you never stood up since?

TUCKER I wanted peace! Deedee, this is not the place. (*To the others*) I apologize for both of us.

DEEDEE I will not be apologized for! All right! The fish-monger's daughter is a fishwife at heart. Apologize for yourself!

TUCKER (*To* CAMILLA) I do.

CAMILLA There's no need. I understand.

DEEDEE I refuse to be understood by you! You're so generous with your apologies, Tucker. Why do you omit the one person to whom you should apologize?

TUCKER I don't think I have.

DEEDEE I do.

TUCKER Don't push me, Deedee.

DEEDEE I demand it!
(*He takes an angry step toward her, a second, then turns to* AARON)

TUCKER I apologize.

AARON Why? What for?

DEEDEE (*Overlapping*) Tucker!

CAMILLA (*Simultaneously*) An apology to me is an apology to Aaron, Tucker. That's enough. (TUCKER *and* AARON *are staring at one another*) TUCKER, THAT'S ENOUGH!
(*The stare continues until:*)

LILY Oh, Aaron, honey!

NORMA Mother!

AARON I don't have a father, Mr. Grogan. I never did.

TUCKER You mean you never knew him.

AARON That's the same thing, isn't it? And he never knew me—which means he never had me for a son. But a mother, I do have. Which is one parent more than most people have.
(DEEDEE *starts for the house as:*)

TUCKER I always thought it was women who defeated me.

DEEDEE (*At the door*) No one has ever defeated you, neither man *nor* woman. You're too *weak*. You and that— (*Pointing*

to LILY) —Flowering Judas. (*Front*) It's the weak who inherit the earth. (*To* SCHUYLER) If you want to get that girl, be
my son, not your father's.

TUCKER Yes. Get what you want. Your mother always has.

DEEDEE Have I? That outcast of a woman there, that "heroine," she's the one who got what she wanted. I got my blue
hair, my pearls . . . and I got you.
(*She goes in. Loud drumming and* CARY *comes out another door*)

CARY Dinner! Dinner!

LILY Hooray! Momma always used to say there's nothing like
good food for bad tempers. Dinner, everybody. Boys, Norma,
Camilla honey—dinner is served!
(*She exits with* CARY, NORMA, SCHUYLER)

CAMILLA (*To* TUCKER) I'm glad I loved you.

TUCKER You always were a nice girl. But sometimes it's better
never than late, isn't it?

CAMILLA Well, the world doesn't stand and wait for some
man to catch up. And people who enjoy this world, they
don't stand and wait either—not even for someone they
loved.

AARON (*Front*) Just pretend I'm not here.

CAMILLA I'll get to you in a minute.

128

TUCKER   I feel as though all evening I've been missing trains.

CAMILLA   Maybe there's still one if you hurry.
    (*She breaks off, for* SCHUYLER *has entered*)

SCHUYLER   Would you come inside and take Mother in to
    dinner?

TUCKER   Schuyler?

SCHUYLER   Yes, sir?

TUCKER   I suppose I'm what my generation calls a "lady's
    man." Well, that's hardly a surprise. But maybe they also
    call us that because a lady's man finds it difficult to com-
    municate with other men. I don't know how to flatter men,
    Schuyler, so I don't know how to reach them.

SCHUYLER   You just talk to them, Father.

TUCKER   And say what? "Hello, how are you?" . . . How
    are *you,* Schuyler? Tell me . . . tell me what you want
    me to do.

SCHUYLER   You've just done it.

TUCKER   It isn't that easy.

SCHUYLER   It is.

TUCKER   Well! (*Touches him, then:*) But now what do I do?

(*Looks at him*) Schuyler, are you still too young to know what too late means? You make sure you never know.
(*Goes in*)

SCHUYLER (*To* CAMILLA) I will. I'll surprise even myself— (NORMA *enters during this. He stops, aware of her, and turns to her with a smile*) I found the ring.

AARON What ring?

SCHUYLER Our engagement ring.

AARON Who says she wants it?

NORMA (*Front*) At last! It's finally about me!

CAMILLA (*Front*) Excuse me. (*To them*) Excuse me. Let any one of you marry or not marry, whatever you want. But, just one minute. (*To* AARON) Don't let it be because of me. His mother's greatest strength is finding everyone's greatest weakness. She said I was selfish. I was. Not to have given you a father. And I was selfish to let you love me so much.

AARON I don't love you so much.

CAMILLA Oh, yes you do. I've made a great show of not tying you to me, but I think I may have put a rope around your neck.

AARON There's no rope on me.

CAMILLA Are you sure?

AARON   No rope.

CAMILLA (*Ruffles his hair, then turns to* NORMA, *very offhand:*)
Pick whoever you want.
        (*And she goes into the house*)

NORMA (*To* AARON)   You don't believe in rings.

AARON (*Front, coming off the deck; the lights coming down
    with him so there is only a soft evening glow on the deck
    and a moonlit pool below*)   How many times have I said
    I don't want to get married? A man can say it till he's blue
    in the face but there isn't a woman on earth who believes
    him.

NORMA (*Coming down to him*)   Oh, yes there is! You never
    want to marry?

AARON   Oh, sure, but only once.

NORMA   When?

AARON   When I'm ready to have other children.

NORMA   And you're not in love with me?

AARON   In only twenty-four hours how could I be sure?

NORMA (*Front*)   How conventional men are!

SCHUYLER (*Coming down to* NORMA)   I'm sure.

                                                    131

AARON (*To* NORMA)   Are you sure what you want?

SCHUYLER (*To* NORMA)   I'll make you sure.
      (*He puts the ring on her finger*)

AARON (*Backing off into the darkness*)   Be sure, Norma, just
be sure.

NORMA (*To* SCHUYLER)   You know what people do when
they fall in love.

SCHUYLER   We get married.

NORMA   And have honeymoons.

SCHUYLER   And children.

NORMA   How many?

SCHUYLER   Three.

NORMA   Where?

SCHUYLER   Connecticut. (*She yawns, puts her hand to her
mouth, horrified—and returns the ring*) But it's his mother
you admire, not him. (*Music starts*) And both of them are
summer people. Not for winter. Not for all year round.
      (NORMA *runs onto the deck looking for* AARON. SCHUYLER
      follows)

NORMA   Plumber? Plumber?

SCHUYLER You can't live as you please very long. You can't stay young!

NORMA Plumber?
(AARON *appears at the edge of the deck. The music grows louder. He holds out his arms to her and she turns to him*)

SCHUYLER Norma, he's still shorter than you are! (*She takes off her shoes.* AARON *begins swaying to the music, encouraging her to come to him*) You have to be safe someplace! You never will be with him! (*Slowly, she goes to* AARON. *He takes her hands and they start to dance, awkwardly at first with small, tentative steps. Then the steps get bigger and smoother and freer as the music swirls louder and fuller*) NORMA, I LOVE YOU!
(*But she doesn't hear, for she is dancing exultantly with* AARON *and they waltz off into the darkness, the music waltzing away with them. Light begins to come up on the deck as* SCHUYLER *picks up one of* NORMA's *shoes, and* LILY's *voice is heard as she comes on:*)

LILY Children, we are waiting on you! Norma? Schuy— (*She sees* SCHUYLER *holding the shoe forlornly. Slowly, she takes it from him*) I don't understand anything any more. All that thunder, all that lightning—and then, it doesn't rain. And now look! (*Pointing with the shoe*) A piece of the moon . . . She isn't coming back.

SCHUYLER (*Sitting on the edge of the deck*) No.

LILY But he isn't going to accept his father.

SCHUYLER No.

LILY Why? Why, Schuyler? (*He shakes his head and leans back, stretching out in a position similar to that* NORMA *was in earlier when she was asleep*) And don't tell me any nonsense about bells ringing. Bells don't ring and people don't open strange doors that might lead anywhere. Not people *we* know! She'll be back. You wait and see. I'm her mother and I— (*But she suddenly presses the shoe to her cheek. A moment, then she looks up and walks to her "bugling" position, saying:*) There's the moon again . . . There: it's gone again.

(*Softly, she begins to hum "Taps" as* CAMILLA *comes out and picks up the other shoe. Light glows around her as:*)

CAMILLA (*Front*) I told you: anybody can do it! Everything's changing so fast, who knows? Maybe someday West Point will be a dancing school! . . . My, that ocean looks pretty! But the tide's coming in and the evening's over. (*To the house*) Good night. (*To* SCHUYLER, *as she comes down the deck steps*) Good night. (*Starts to kiss him, catches herself and smiles at the audience:*) Good night.

(*And she starts off*)

The Curtain Falls